# UNSHAKEABLE

## A Hope-Filled Devotional For Police Wives Facing An Anti-Cop World

LEAH EVERLY

# DEDICATION

This book is dedicated to all those whose lives have been lost due to the war on cops. I am so grateful for all the sacrifices you made trying to make this world a better place. You are not forgotten.

# BONUS

Dislike writing in books? Me too!

Download your free printable workbook plus other helpful resources for each chapter by going to:

loveandbluesblog.com/unshakeable

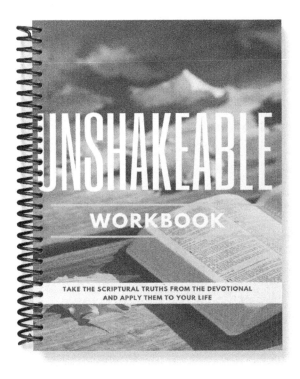

# CONTENTS

# IN THIS WORLD YOU WILL HAVE TROUBLE

*I have told you these things, so that in me you may have peace.*
*In this world you will have trouble.*
*But take heart! I have overcome the world.*
*John 16:33*

My spiritual journey as a law enforcement wife has been a wild ride. After my husband was unceremoniously ousted from the small-town department he had first been hired, I was ready to say good-bye. Everything about that experience was so wrong, so unfair, that I was over it. I figured - okay, we tried. He did the law enforcement thing, and maybe that's all he was meant to do. I was just fine with living a quiet, law enforcement-free life. For my husband's sake, I hoped he could continue to live his dream, but as for me, I was okay with moving on.

It wasn't long afterward, however, that I felt the pull to start blogging: and not just any blog, but a blog specifically for law enforcement wives. It didn't make much (read: any) sense to me, but the impression from God was unmistakable. Blogging was what I was supposed to do, so tentatively, I gave it a shot, even though I questioned Him basically the entire time.

In the four years I've spent working on *Love and Blues*, I've questioned God on whether I should be doing it or not at least once a month. Those small doubts have been met with gentle nudges. At times when I've been hugely in doubt, when I've said, "Nope! I'm done, and I'm shutting it all down," He has sent me unequivocal signs to keep going.

One of these times was the first September after I started. I had prayed for an unmistakable sign to continue, and if I didn't receive one, I was going to sign up for a court reporting course and move on with my life. That evening, my post *How To Survive The War On Cops As A Police Wife* went viral and nearly crashed my site because I had a sudden influx of traffic that was approximately 2000% what I had had before. I took that as my unequivocal sign and kept going.

The year after that, I published *The Proverbs 31 Police Wife*, which was actually done without as much celebration as you might think. I was terrified of doing so. So terrified, in fact, that the night before it was set to publish, I considered tanking the whole project. Even though I'd finished it completely, even though it was completely ready to go, even though I had promoted it and gotten plenty of pre-orders and all of that, I wanted to let it all go. I cried on the bathroom floor that night, asking God if I could undo it. I asked if I live more quietly, not drawing attention to myself, not doing anything that might provoke any sort of attacks.

I ultimately got to a place of, "I'll do it. And whether I sink or whether I swim, I'll trust you." In all honesty, I was more emotionally prepared to sink than swim. I fitfully slept that night and was in a state of anxiety the following week, but God saw me through that, too. That book has resulted in more emails than I can count from readers thanking me for my testimony and strengthening them through unimaginable trials. I have come to understand why He wanted me to push past the uncertainty, and I'm beyond grateful for it.

There have been so many signs just like that, and yet it wasn't until last year that we got the impression that my husband was destined to return to law enforcement. There were little, continual nudges from the Holy Spirit that probably could have been ignored, if not for one completely undeniable answer from God last Spring.

At the time, my husband was in Washington D.C. for his father's interment in Arlington National Cemetery. He found himself with some down time during the week and decided to take a trip to the National Law Enforcement Museum. While he was there, he prayed whether he should return to law enforcement or not. Shortly thereafter, his phone rang. I called him, saying, "Hey, this is really weird, but I got this impression like you'll be back at the academy soon."

Seriously, I was driving with my kids, and had gotten lost near where he had previously attended the academy when I had an unmistakeable whisper from the Holy Ghost telling me that very thing. It was so jarring I had to tell him about it. Obviously I didn't know about his prayer, so we were both floored. There was no denying what had happened in that moment.

We were so excited. I supposed this was the reason I had continued writing a blog for law enforcement wives. Maybe I needed keep the faith that he would be back someday. At that moment, he committed himself to his part to return, trusting that God would do the rest. Even though I found myself a little nervous, I was happy that he could continue to pursue his dream.

However, now that we have hit what feels like a new phase in the war on cops, those feelings are a little different. After all, the excitement of the prospect of my husband returning to law enforcement has been replaced with a certain amount of dread. Now our prayers sound a little more like, "Wait... Really?" Because of the current political climate and social attitude toward law enforcement, the fear and uncertainty of being married to a law enforcement officer is hitting me like never before. I think that's true of every single law enforcement wife, unless they've been living in a well-constructed bubble.

Police officers are being criticized like never before. They are being accused of being horrendously racist, unnecessarily shooting and killing people of color. They're accused of being trigger-happy pigs who shoot without thought and without remorse. At best, they're being labeled unnecessary, with many people shouting to defund all police departments, saying the community could do a better job.

On the flipside, if police don't respond in the way the news media think is best, they are labeled as ineffective. When they walk more softly, worried about being demonized and, as a result, don't prevent a crime from happening, there are screams of,

"Why didn't they do something?" It's very much a no-win situation.

The news media spins every police shooting into something it's not. Facts are manipulated or outright ignored to fit a larger narrative, which only fuels the fire. If you deign to point these facts out, you are called all kinds of horrible names. You are accused of condoning the worst kinds of evil. As a result, you eventually stop trying to speak truth. Instead, you sit in silent terror, seething with fury at the injustice around you, feeling helpless to do anything about it.

Police officers are being targeted for murder, and nobody seems to care. Police officers find themselves facing criminal prosecution for doing their job, even if all evidence points to a justified shooting. Any use of force, frankly, is seen as excessive by the world at large. If police officers take down evil people using anything except their words, criticisms roll in. Cops are seen as the enemy, and the real bad guys are being seen as heroes and martyrs. It feels like the world is completely backward.

What's more anxiety-inducing, though, is that the anti-cop attitude is no longer restricted to a few on the fringes of society. It's not just crazy strangers who are putting forth the opinion that "ACAB" (all cops are bad/bastards, depending on who's saying it.) You are also probably finding your friends and family have begun to be taken in by the mob mentality. Maybe not all of them, but enough.

Even when your loved ones say to you, "not all cops", you still hear the hidden implication of, "…but most cops." You scroll through your news feed and see those you love spreading misinformation that works to endanger your officer's life, even if they then turn around and tell you, "We're praying for your officer." It's all you can do not to punch them in the face.

You find yourself hurt by the callousness of the world. You are terrified of what could happen to your officer every time he leaves the house. You worry about your kids being bullied because their father is a police officer. It's hard enough for you to feel afraid of the future, but you wish your kids didn't have to face that uncertainty. You lay awake at night worried about the prospect of being a single parent.

You wonder if your officer should even be in law enforcement anymore, and maybe wonder how you can talk him out of the uniform and into a nice, safe job as a banker or something. Maybe you've already had discussions about that very thing. Where an on-the-job death seemed like a possibility before, it now begins to feel like an eventuality you must mentally prepare for.

In the meantime, you are forced to stay silent. If you choose to say anything in defense of law enforcement, if you say anything that exposes the current insanity of the world, if you dare bring facts into a battle of emotions, you are vilified. Publicly. Probably by multiple people. Possibly all at the same time.

Those who do so might even consist of your friends or members of your own family. Even then, it feels like they will do anything they can to make you seem like the bad guy, even if they should know better. You risk being ostracized from the very people who mean the most to you, which makes you feel even lonelier at a time you so desperately need their love and support.

For the record, this is not how I would have planned to start a devotional. I would love to lift you up from the get-go, but there is no denying this is where we are. I know it, you know it, and we need to acknowledge it; because I don't know about you, but I am tired of staying silent. I am tired of feeling powerless. I want to meet you where you are by recognizing the most painful things you face right now. I want to lead you to the ultimate source of love and support so you can heal those things.

We were promised trouble in this world, and this definitely looks like trouble. Yet, as evil as this world is, Christ promised He has already overcome it. Even though we live in dark times, you can take heart because you follow a Savior who has seen what was to come - every little bit of it. None of this comes as a surprise to Him. He personally experienced and carried the weight of all the awfulness the world has to offer, including the trials you face right now.

Remember, Christ did that for the entire world, but also for you personally. He is not only the Light of the World[1], but is also your personal light in the darkness. He is the only One you can unfailingly rely on when everything else seems to crumble away. He knows you, He loves you, and He is anxiously waiting to help light your way in what can seem like an impenetrably dark time.

In this devotional, I want to guide you to the scriptural truths that will encourage you. I want you to know you are not alone. God is with you, and so is a whole blue line family who is facing the same storm. I want to help you find the strength from the

---

[1] John 8:12

Lord that is necessary to keep your sanity in all the roles you take on: as a Christian, as a police wife, as a mother, and in every other role you have been called to take on.

Through Him, you can find the courage to love and support your husband, no matter where your journey takes you after this. You can find the wisdom you need to guide your children and inspire them to face scary situations with confidence and bravery. You can be strengthened to love, forgive, and pray for your enemies, even those who do the most harm to you and your family. You can gain the tenacity to stand for truth, even if you have to stand alone.

This is not an easy road to walk. Living as a Christian in such a fallen world is usually not easy, nor is living as a police family. When you combine the two, you find yourself walking a particularly tough path. Unfortunately, God never said it would be easy. In fact, He said you would more than likely be hated on His behalf.

However, in this circumstance and always, He is with you. He sees the tears you cry. He sees you when you are a ball of anxiety scrolling through your newsfeed, seeing death threats and hatred from the other side. He sees your anxiety when your family is specifically targeted, whether through acts of violence or property damage like slashed tires. He sees you when you get angry at the state of the world and all the unfairness it brings your way. He sees when you get tempted (or even do - understandably) hurl insults and darkness back. He sees the demons you face. He understands, perfectly.

No matter what trouble this world brings you, I want to show you scriptural evidence that you can and will get through this. I want to lead you through your questions and doubts to the God who is with you, every single step of the way.

This is not easy.

With God on your side, however, **you are unstoppable.**

# AUTHOR'S NOTE

As with my other devotionals, I have included prayer ideas at the end of each section to help you start the conversation with your Heavenly Father.

There is also a free printable workbook and other online resources to help you make the most of the devotional available at loveandbluesblog.com/unshakeable . Be sure to check it out, especially if you hate writing in books.

That being said, if you like notating books, I tried to leave plenty of space throughout for you to write your thoughts. I hope it helps!

# THERE IS ANOTHER IN THE FIRE

*He answered and said,*
*Lo, I see four men loose, walking in the midst of the fire,*
*and they have no hurt;*
*and the form of the fourth is like the Son of God.*
*Daniel 3:25*

A few years ago, it seemed like there were only sparks of hatred against the police. I never would have dreamed that they would have grown into the inferno we find ourselves living in now. Every day, fuel is added to the fire by the media who is quick to make a quick buck by promoting a false narrative. The truth does not matter anymore, and it does nothing to slow the spread. People, even the best of people, are taken in by these news outlets and spread that narrative, contributing their own kindling to the fire.

Dissenters are quickly and brutally quelled, with supporters not allowing for any quenching of the fire. The accusations, the insults, the widespread societal acceptance of being anti-law enforcement, they all blaze forward, consuming everything in their path. At times, the fiery opposition feels like it might swallow you, your officer, and your family whole.

Maybe that's why the story of Shadrach, Meshach, and Abednego speaks so strongly to me right now.

In their time, King Nebuchadnezzar had set up a golden idol which all his officials were commanded to worship. Anyone who refused was sentenced to be thrown in a furnace. When informed that Shadrach, Meshach, and Abednego had refused to bow down to the idol, he commanded that they be thrown into the furnace. Not just any furnace, though, but one that was turned up seven times hotter than usual, making escape basically unthinkable.

Before their execution, they were given one last chance to bow down before the idol. They refused, responding, "God can save us. But if He does not, we still will not serve your gods.[2]"

That statement sends shivers up my spine. They were so strong in their faith that they willingly entered the fire rather than bowing to false idols - even if God decided not to save them. They knew in their hearts that God had the power to do so, but would surrender to whatever He had in mind for them.

As you would expect, the king cast them into the furnace. However, the three men were miraculously unharmed. The king

---

[2] Daniel 3:17-18

14

saw something else: incredibly, there were four men, not three, in the fire. They all walked around in the flames without being burned. The fourth man was described as looking like the Son of God.

Because of their faith, these men were not only protected from the flames, but also accompanied by Christ during their trial. When I try to imagine what they felt when they learned for sure their faith had not been misplaced, I am amazed. I imagine they had a mind-blowing conversation in that furnace, one they would not have had if they had backed down from the challenge of the king.

There are a lot of good parallels to take away from this story and apply to your current situation.

First of all, think about the courage of Shadrach, Meshach, and Abednego. The prospect of entering the fiery furnace must have been terrifying. I can't help but wonder if they considered, even for a moment, renouncing their faith to save themselves from that fate. Even when faced with that fear, however, they were much more afraid of denying God.

They had faith in God's power, and knew that the decision they made mattered. If they acquiesced to the king's request, they knew they might save themselves temporarily, but would be letting down their God. They made the decision that the fear of the furnace was nothing compared to what would happen if they turned their backs on God. They wouldn't let the fear of the world draw them away from doing what they knew was right - no matter what happened. They even acknowledged that they might die from that decision, and made their peace with it. That's faith.

This is especially true when you consider that they were not immediately rescued from their predicament. God could have done any number of things to save them: put out the fire, made the furnace malfunction, prevent the guards from throwing them in, blocking the entrance, or any number of other possibilities. He instead chose to let the guards make the choice to throw them into the fire, but kept them protected from the flames. He let them go all the way, relying on their faith the whole way. He showed them His power by protecting them and being present with them in their trial.

Similarly, the fire you face as a police wife is terrifying. No, your outcome is not as certain as being thrown into a furnace, but you see the riots. Whether you live in the heart of the riots or are more removed from them, you have seen the damage they have caused. You see how out-of-control the opposition has become.

Sending your officer out into such a world can make you feel like you're going to have a heart attack until he returns home safely - though even then, you can't help but wonder if he will end up the next YouTube sensation. While the outcome is not as certain as them being told "worship the idol or you're going into the fire", you know without a doubt that the hatred against police puts your officer and everyone associated with him in more danger.

No matter what you are called to do, whether that is convincing your husband to leave law enforcement, whether it's standing firm and continuing to support his position on the thin blue line, or whatever else God is calling you to do, you will find yourself having to make a choice. You will have to decide whether you will bow down and worship a false idol or continue steadfastly toward God. Nobody knows what that personal choice will look like but you, and nobody can make the choice for you. You must decide. Are you able to utter the phrase, "God will save us - and if He does not, I still will not worship the way you're asking me to."

There are so many things to be afraid of, I know. Ultimately, however, they pale in comparison to backing down from what God wants you to do. It's much scarier to think of not living the life God wants you to live because you were too afraid to do so. It is scary to think about what it would be like to have to look back on your life and discover you have fallen short of what He expected of you.

If you are doing what God has asked of you, He will no doubt open doors for you. He will give both of you the wisdom and discernment you need to navigate the world of law enforcement safely. You and your officer can be put in the right place at the right time to avoid unnecessary trouble. He might give you a heads up about something otherwise unknowable that protects you from danger. He can comfort you when you need it.

However, let's get back to that statement of, "even if He does not."

Let's face it, even though God has all power, He may not choose to remove the troubles facing law enforcement. You may face trouble personally, whether it's a matter of property damage, personal injury, or even death. There is no way to sugarcoat this: I don't know what God has in store for you and your family.

Nobody does, and I can't guarantee rainbows and sunshine from here on out. Actually, I can pretty much guarantee it will *not* be rainbows and sunshine. Danger almost certainly lies ahead for everyone who moves forward steadfastly in Christ, especially those who stand for justice, truth, law, and order.

Unfortunately, no matter how strong your faith is, no matter how good of a person you and your officer are, bad things happen. God can do all things, but sometimes He chooses not to. You know as well as I do that all too often, the people who are hurt or killed by others are some of the ones who least deserve it. Some of the most unfair things happen to the best people. Sometimes the best things happen to those who don't deserve it. Some days, everything feels completely upside down, backwards, and inside out. Those disparities can make you doubt the goodness of God at times. That is understandable when you don't see the whole plan. That is where faith has to come in.

Faith means choosing to believe that this choice is not based on God's indifference toward you, but is instead the choice of a loving Father who knows ultimately what is best for you. It means believing that even if it results in excruciating pain, He has things in store that can only be accomplished through that pain. It means finding a way to trust that He would not inflict more pain on you than is necessary to grow you into who you are meant to be.

It is hard to understand God's goodness when He chooses not to intervene. It's hard not to feel anxious when you realize that He may choose not to intervene for you or your officer - that even if you are faithful and do everything right, the things you most fear could certainly come to pass. In those circumstances, your faith is even more important. See, while God knows and sees more than we do, it's more important in those uncertain moments to cling tight to Him. To pray to Him, to seek His face, and to ask the questions only He can provide the answers to.

God can always be trusted. God is always good. Even when life feels horrible and unfair, He is always in control. Even when the lives of good officers are lost. Even when it appears that evil wins and the criminal is getting away. It may appear that way at times, but it is not true. If God says He will never leave us, He will never leave us. If God says He will work all things for our good, He will do just that. God's promises are real. Whether we see them playing out on this side of life or not, that truth is unchangeable.

Even in the times where life seems the most out of control, when everything seems to be going wrong, God is there. He is still in control. He has not left you and never will.

Choose to lift your eyes up from the fire that licks at your feet and focus instead on the Most High God. Look forward with an eye of faith to your eternal reward. Keep striving forward with that in mind, not concerning yourself with what people can do - because man is nothing compared to God. If God's power can part the Red Sea, shake prison walls, cause powerful earthquakes, mighty storms, and floods that cover the whole earth, that power can carry you through whatever Satan throws at you during the war on cops. Trust that He will do things for your good, all the time - even when they don't seem good.

Have the unwavering faith of Shadrach, Meshach, and Abednego to believe He is strong enough to save you, but that even if He doesn't, He has better plans in store for you. Have the faith required to say that even if everything goes wrong, you will still bow down and worship only Him. Have faith that God can, but also echo what Christ said in the Garden of Gethsemane: "not my will, but Thine be done.[3]"

In every circumstance, God has your back. Choose to move forward through the flames with confidence, knowing that even in the heat of a fiery furnace, you can be kept safe - but even if not, He is still with you, today and always.

---

[3] Luke 22:42

# PRAYER IDEAS

- Thank God for His presence with you in the fire.
- Talk to God frankly about what you are afraid of.  Be open and honest with Him, holding nothing back.
- Ask God to help you see the times when He has been with you in trials before to help strengthen you for this and future trials.
- Ask for help in developing the faith you need to be true to Him under any and all circumstances.

# THEY HATED CHRIST FIRST

*If the world hates you, keep in mind that it hated me first.*
*John 15:18*

From the moment Christ was conceived, He was scorned. After all, He was born to an unwed mother. That fact alone put him at the bottom of the social pyramid 2000 years ago. You can hardly blame Joseph for considering quietly divorcing Mary when he learned of her pregnancy. Thank goodness Joseph listened to the angel who told him the truth of the matter[4]. He married her anyway, standing behind her in her incredible calling, acting in faith as Christ's earthly father.

Even on the day of Christ's birth, King Herod tried to have Him killed. To keep Him safe, Mary and Joseph were forced to flee to Egypt. They were only able to return to Israel after the

---

[4] Matthew 1:19

death of King Herod[5]. Even then, however, I suspect Satan was already working on stirring up the hearts of people in the final plot against Him. After all, he knew what Christ was sent to do. He wasn't about to let that happen without at least throwing a few bumps in the road.

When Christ was grown, He was tempted by Satan in the wilderness[6]. Satan tried to get Him to test God by throwing Himself off a tall building, tried to get Him to turn rocks to bread to prove His power, and promised all kinds of things in exchange for worshiping him. Even in the face of all this temptation, Christ chose to continue to follow God anyway. He knew what He had been sent to do and trusted fully in God's promises.

Even with the many miracles He performed and the many good works He did, Christ was continually criticized by the Pharisees. There was no shortage of complaints about Him. He was slammed for sharing the table with tax collectors and sinners[7]. He was slandered, being called a glutton and a drunkard[8]. He was criticized for healing on the Sabbath, with His critics saying He was breaking the Sabbath by doing so[9]. Around every corner, there was someone testing him, trying to trip Him up and show evidence that He wasn't actually the Son of God.

Of course, the final insult to Christ was the plot to kill Him. The Pharisees hated someone who lived a perfect life - the only

---

[5] Matthew 2:13
[6] Matthew 4:1-11
[7] Matthew 9:11
[8] Matthew 11:19
[9] Mark 3:1-6

person to ever perform such a feat, by the way. Regardless of all the good He did, they sought to destroy him as soon as they possibly could. They stirred up an angry mob who were so blinded by hatred and offense that they ultimately chose Barabbas to be released over Christ. Pilate acquiesced to the angry mob. You might see parallels to this particular situation playing out right now, too. After all, there are plenty of politicians trying to appease the angry mob by persecuting good officers in our day - but I digress.

The hatred was not fair, but it undeniably existed. Even so, He chose not to let his dissenters get in the way of doing what He was sent to do. He went bravely forward, even though He knew what was to come. Regardless of the opposition He faced, however, He undauntedly continued to perform God's work. He was sustained by knowing where His loyalties belonged.

Christ submitted Himself to the worst kind of torture imaginable. He experienced pains none of us could ever imagine. I mean, think about all the pain that exists in just one life, then think: he went through the pain of every single life that has ever or will ever exist. He did so with the end in mind, however. He knew that by standing in the line of fire for us, He could pay for each of our sins. Because He Himself had never sinned, He was the only one who could stand in our place. He suffered through everything we would ever suffer through because He loves us so much. He wanted to be able to better understand and succor us. He wanted us to be able to be redeemed.

Incredibly, Christ even paid the price for His executioners. He asked for them to be forgiven, even as they were in the act of taking His life[10]. They didn't ask for it or appreciate it at the time, but Christ distinguished himself by always choosing to do the right thing. He did what was asked of Him, no matter how difficult it was, no matter whether it was appreciated or not, because He knew who He truly served with His actions.

It is more important than ever to think about how Christ lived and how those around Him responded. When the world around you holds all law enforcement officers in such contempt, you can take comfort in remembering that they hated Christ first.

This is especially important when it comes to your officer. Now, I am not saying your husband is perfect by any means. He is still undeniably human. He has made and will continue to make mistakes. He probably has that dark cop humor that makes you say, "That's not funny," while laughing hysterically anyway (no? Just me?). Your officer probably errs on the side of jadedness about humanity, even though, at heart, he truly loves people and wants to help them. He's annoyingly finicky about where he sits in restaurants and gets the side-eye from servers when he makes you move. He probably annoys you deeply when he points out traffic violations while out on date night - whether you let him know how annoying it is or not.

That being said, you know your husband's heart. You know how much it hurts him when things go wrong on shift. You've been there to hold him after a call in which he did everything right, yet everything went wrong, when he finds himself questioning every action he took, wondering if he could have

---

[10] Luke 23:34

done more. You've found him awake in the middle of the night, unable to sleep because of the scenes replaying in his head. You've seen the times he's come home, silently wrapped the kids in a hug, and walked off because he needs a minute to collect himself. You may never have had the nerve to ask what exactly it was that made him fall apart like that, but you know how much it affects him. You know how seriously he takes his responsibilities, how much the job has changed him.

That knowledge is exactly why the hatred of law enforcement feels so desperately unfair. When people call him and everyone in the same profession a bastard, it rankles you because you know the truth about police officers, but especially about the man you married. When people accuse him of being a power-hungry jerk, you know how untrue it is, because you have walked him through all the small choices that led to big actions. You know what I know - that if the cop haters truly understood even a shred of what he went through each day, they would feel differently. You know the true weight of the badge he wears and the toll it takes on him. You know his heart. It is painful to know that others wish him harm for a job he gives so much of himself to.

It's also terrifying. You have to send your love out into such a world that hates him, not knowing if he will be able to make it home. I mean, you've always known that was a possibility. You knew that dreaded knock on the door could happen any time. You have probably mentally rehearsed it a time or two, especially on those days where he was late and forgot to let you know. It just didn't feel quite so inevitable a possibility as it does now. Before, it was more the possibility of a line-of-duty death because someone tries to shoot him to get away. Now, you also have the added risk of him being ambushed simply because he's a police officer as a part of the greater trend of riots against law enforcement. His uniform that you are so proud of has become a target on his back.

As case law and legislation changes, fear of civil and criminal prosecution of your officer has become a reality. This is the case even for actions that would have been seen before as a legitimate use of force. That means that not only do you have to worry about on the job injury or death, but also that your officer could end up in jail with the very people he's sent there. That's a lot to take.

Being a police wife is about a hundred times scarier when it feels like the whole world hates law enforcement. It's not fair that your husband is judged so harshly. It's not right that you should have so many scary things to worry about. There is one thing, however, that makes all of this a little more manageable, and that is the fact that your officer is not the first.

Your officer is not the first to be hated for doing what God has called him to do. He is not the first to have people suspect his motivations, even when he commits himself to doing things the right way. He is not the first man to ever be slandered and misrepresented. He is not the first to be taken for granted. He's definitely not the first to be treated unfairly.

Keep in mind that Christ understands all too well what those in law enforcement are facing right now. He, too, has been unfairly under fire, even when He did everything right. He also knew that days would come when others who follow Him and choose the course of righteousness and justice would be persecuted, too - which is exactly why He warned us about it so clearly.

No matter what changes happen in the world, no matter who sees your husband as someone he isn't, Christ sees him as he really is. Christ understands your officer better than anyone else. He knows very well what a difference your officer and the rest of the blue line make in the world.

Every time your husband puts himself on the line to protect others, God is there. He sees every time your officer runs toward danger while everyone else runs away, and He applauds that bravery. Especially when He sees your officer's fear and his choice to do the right thing anyway. He hears your husband every time he cries out in prayer. If he prays for help, God is always there and willing to help. If it's out of anger, He is there to help dissipate the anger and lead your officer to peace. If the prayers come because he is devastated about what he has seen or dealt with, God is there to catch every one of his tears.

God sees the reality of why your husband and his fellow officers do what they do, having seen every interaction from start to finish. He doesn't have to look at things through the short-sighted and biased lens of YouTube videos or the media. He celebrates every success and is there to comfort in every misstep. He is the only one who knows precisely what your husband goes through.

God is the only one who knows your officer's heart perfectly. He sees all the things your officer does, knows about all the things he will never be able to talk about, and He will never forget them. The good things your husband does will eventually be rewarded. You may have small rewards on earth, but more than likely will receive that reward in Heaven. The unfair things that are done against your husband and your family will be made right a hundred times over.

Having this perspective helps keep you out of a lot of unnecessary arguments and keeps you from a lot of unnecessary hurt.

Whenever you see police being decried as villains, you have to focus on the God who knows your husband's heart: the God who watched His own son be treated in such a way, and allowed it to happen for the good of all mankind. Remember that one day, if you and your officer continue doing what you're supposed to do, no matter what danger comes your way, you will be welcomed into His arms with pride[11].

Choose your battles wisely, and remember: Your husband isn't the first man the world has hated.

---

[11] Matthew 10:22

# PRAYER IDEAS

- Thank God for sending His son to pay for your sins. Thank Him for that unimaginable sacrifice.

- Express gratitude for the deep understanding He has as you stand beside your husband in turbulent times.

- Ask for help seeing what you can learn from the circumstances you find yourself in.

- Ask for peace in your heart as you navigate a difficult world.

# FOR SUCH A TIME AS THIS

*Who knows whether you have not come to the kingdom*
*for such a time as this?*
*Esther 4:14 (ESV)*

Look around you for a moment. Of all the times in history you could have been born, you are here. Think about the significance of that. You were born in this time, with your particular parents, with your particular struggles, and with all the struggles and advantages that this time comes with. God could have placed you anytime, anywhere. Yet, He, in all His wisdom, has placed you here. You find yourself in the middle of the most heated conflict that has ever really existed regarding law enforcement in the United States. You are here in the role of a police wife - for better or for worse.

Think about that. God is all-knowing and all-seeing. He

created you. He knows the number of hairs on your head[12]. He knew you from your mother's womb[13]. With the immense amount of information He has about you, He decided you were supposed to come to Earth to where you are today. If you have faith in all that, it follows naturally that He must have put you here with a specific purpose in mind. A God who is that deliberate in the most minute details does not do things casually or by accident. I think all that information together says something about how much God believes in your ability to get through the current situation.

One example of a woman who was put in a particular place and time for a significant reason was Esther. Esther was a Jew born in Shushan, the capital of Persia[14]. At that time, the Jews were in captivity and exile. However, when King Ahasuerus of Persia banished his Queen, he needed another to take her place. The virgins of the kingdom were to be presented to him[15], and he chose Esther to be his queen. The King was not aware she was a Jew, of course. Esther's cousin, Mordecai, had instructed her to keep her heritage a secret[16].

This relationship played a pivotal role later in preventing the assassination of the king. When the plot to Mordecai's attention, he was able to inform Esther. She was able to let the King know, and his advisers thwarted the attempt in time to save his life[17]. By

---

[12] Luke 12:7
[13] Jeremiah 1:5
[14] Esther 2:5-7
[15] Esther 2:2
[16] Esther 2:10
[17] Esther 2:22

doing this, Esther undoubtedly gained the King's trust.

This trust became extremely important when one of the King's advisers convinced him to issue an order that all the Jews in the empire were to be annihilated[18]. Her cousin Mordecai implored her to persuade the King to rescind the order, but she was scared to do so.

The reason Esther was scared is that nobody was supposed to go see the King without being called. She risked certain death by doing so. She was also very aware of what had happened to the queen who preceded her. The King already had a track record of banishing his queens for displeasing him, so it seemed reasonable to assume he would probably do the same to her.

Mordecai encouraged her to do so in spite of that fear. He told Esther:

> "If you keep silent at this time, relief and deliverance will rise for the Jews from another place, but you and your father's house will perish. And who knows whether you have not come to the kingdom for such a time as this?"[19]

When God promised deliverance to the Jews of Persia, He meant it. He knew it would happen with or without Esther's help. If Esther chose not to do her part, the plan wouldn't be destroyed, only modified. She would also have to take responsibility for that decision, but God will never force us to do

---

[18] Esther 3:13
[19] Esther 4:14, ESV

what He wants. We always have the freedom to choose. However, the question of whether she was put in that place for just that purpose is a really interesting one. After all, she was an unlikely candidate for Queen of Persia. She had undergone a lot of adversity in that position. Maybe it was all for the express purpose of being able to speak for her people.

It turns out, maybe that's exactly the case, since the gamble paid off. Taking the risk of going in to see the King without permission and speaking for her people ended up working. The King rescinded the order and the Jews were saved. Because of her courage, she brought honor to her family and safety to the her people as a whole.

Now, I have no way of knowing whether or not your purpose in life will be as dramatic as Esther's. I don't know the reason God put you here. What I do know, however, is that God undoubtedly placed you here for a reason. Remember: He knows everything. He knows what you are capable of. He knows who He has surrounded you with. He knows whose lives you will touch. He knows who will see you and be strengthened by your example. He knows exactly who you are meant to be. None of these things may present themselves to you in an obvious way like they did Esther. Maybe you will only be aware of these things when you meet Him again after this life. I do, however, know that someday, whether in this life or the next, your reason for existing at this particular point in time will become apparent to you.

One thing that makes your role so crucial right now is your unique position of being in both the "police" and "civilian" camps. While you are a law enforcement supporter with obviously significant stakes in the well-being of the police force, you, too, find yourself on the sidelines. You look at the actions of law enforcement from the point of view of a civilian but are also allowed a glimpse of what your officer faces every day. While being affiliated with law enforcement in this way sometimes makes you a target, it also gives you a perspective that others do not have. By finding common ground between the police and those who have been misled by the media, you can act as a peacemaker. You can work to bridge the gap between people with different opinions. You can do so with grace and dignity, no matter how intense things become.

I am not saying, of course, that you will be able to change the whole world. So much of the anti-police rhetoric has become so ingrained in the media and society that trying to change the opinions of everyone around you is not possible. However, you can be an example of a God-fearing, loving person who also loves law enforcement. Being kind may not overhaul someone's opinion, but spreading love in a world full of hate no doubt plants seeds. God can grow those seeds as He sees fit through the promptings of the Spirit or through additional experiences from others.

Through your example, you may find that who you are helps prevent at least some of the lies from taking root in the heart of someone who might otherwise have been susceptible to them. It might just make them think twice before believing that all cops are bad because they will know you and your officer as good people.

However, being a good example is not always enough. This is especially true when the Enemy is working tirelessly to tear down everything good and noble in society. In this time, you will absolutely find yourself being called to speak for truth. If you find yourself in a position to speak out against the hatred of police officers, remember what Mordecai told Esther: Who knows whether you have come to be in your position as a police wife for such a time as this?

The war on cops may leave you feeling infinitely small. It can make you feel like you must be silent or your whole life will be demolished. I get it. There are a lot of torches and pitchforks going around for anyone who supports law enforcement. Vitriol even comes when you simply question the facts and statistics others spread as truth. That means that when you call these out as falsehoods, you are going to be persecuted even more. It is undoubtedly a scary prospect, but remember: when you speak for truth, you speak for God.

If you're not sure what to say, pray about it. Ask God to give you the words to say in that moment, and He will no doubt help guide you. You might find yourself saying something you did not expect to because the person listening needed it phrased in a particular way to understand it - and God knew that. You might find yourself not saying things you think you should have because He deems them not as essential as other things. Whenever I have done this, I have been pleasantly surprised by how He has guided me. Whether you are called to speak out to thousands or just one, God will use you to spread a message of love and hope if you allow Him to do so.

What you say may not immediately connect with those you're talking to. God may ask you to say things that are difficult for them to hear, and they may respond with vitriol, regardless of whether you needed to say it or not. God will lead you to say and do what He needs you to, but that is not to say things will be all rosy. It may not ever change their minds, but it may strengthen you to speak out again in the future. It may give you the resolve you need to find actionable solutions to make the world a better place. Be open to what God wants, and do not be discouraged if things do not immediately go the way you think they should.

Like Esther, we do not exist solely for our own benefit. Everything we do impacts others. With or without being a ruler, we have the capacity to impact every life intwined with ours. I believe strongly that God knows you can have a positive impact on society in your role, in your own unique way. You have a story and a perspective that's all your own. You have a strength that can both protect and inspire. You have influence on your circle of friends, family, and acquaintances, and He knows what you can do with that. Ultimately, however, you have to choose what you will do with those opportunities.

Being both a Christian and a police wife in this moment requires courage. However, you have to remember that if God placed you here with a particular reason in mind, He knew you would be strong enough to handle it all. He knew things would not be easy, but that you would make it. He knows how the struggles you face will mold you into who you are meant to be. He knows you will be all the better for this. He knows what you can withstand, how far you can go, and He is not going to let you drown under the waves. Remember that, especially when it feels like you are about to drown. This knowledge can give you the strength you need to overcome whatever specific breed of adversity you are facing right now.

I have no idea what you are meant to do in your position. You have unique gifts, talents, advantages, and knowledge that change how you approach life. They can all be used for good somehow, but only God knows how. Similarly, only God knows whether you are meant to do something big or small. Only He knows whether you are called to do one big, sweeping thing or a lot of little things. In all things, God is sovereign. When life is most chaotic, remember that He knows the beginning from the end. He knows why you are here and what you are meant to do. If you continue to seek Him, you will find what that is.

You are more powerful than you may realize. Use that power and influence for good, just like Esther. Do so prayerfully, peacefully, and with the knowledge that God will always guide you to the right things, and you never have to be afraid.

# PRAYER IDEAS

- Thank God for the family, friends, and acquaintances He has given you.
- Express gratitude for knowing what you are capable of.
- Ask how you can speak out and take action in favor of the good.
- Ask how you can speak against evil.
- Ask for God's guidance and protection as you do these things.
- Ask to see the change you make in the world when you feel discouraged.

# KEEP YOUR EYES ON CHRIST

*Peter got down out of the boat, walked on the water and came toward Jesus. But when he saw the wind, he was afraid and, beginning to sink, cried out, "Lord, save me!" Immediately Jesus reached out his hand and caught him. "You of little faith," he said, "why did you doubt?"*
*Matthew 14:30-31*

Like snails in a rainstorm, the anti-police trolls seem to thrive when things are the dreariest. Before you have even properly awakened for the day, your news feed is filled with all kinds of terrible news about law enforcement: from targeted attacks on officers to people decrying another poorly reported police shooting, from the criminalization of law enforcement to the calls for defunding all departments.

There are lies, half-truths, and omissions being made to make law enforcement look like they are bad overall. Out-of-context or absolutely fictitious "facts and figures" are weaponized to make the police look dangerous. There are physical and verbal attacks on you and your officer personally, whether those come in the form of you being followed and harassed or having your personal property damaged or stolen.

Sometimes these attacks come from total strangers when you post something on social media that contains a thin blue line flag or even just uses the tag #BackTheBlue. Sometimes, they come from friends or family who feel like they have completely turned against you, making formerly safe spaces like book clubs, play groups, or other gatherings feel like places you are no longer welcome.

You also contend with the open and unadulterated hatred of police officers from people with influence: politicians, athletes, musicians, and others, many of whom you have probably enjoyed prior to now. You may find yourself wondering if you can even enjoy their work now that you know what they really think of you, when their words strengthen others in their persecution of law enforcement.

It's not surprising that all this leaves your heart feeling heavy. When you are endlessly pelted with negativity from others, it does not come as much of a surprise that you feel isolated and alone. Even having others who are going through the same thing can do little to quell your feelings of despair because standing up and saying so publicly is so difficult. You have to support each other invisibly, behind closed doors, so as not to incite more violence against you.

When you send your officer out into the night, your anxiety

rises higher than it ever has before. You are all too aware of the additional dangers he now has to face, especially if you live in a place that has been hit hardest by the anti-cop rhetoric. More than ever, your sleep is interrupted by nightmares about what could happen to your officer - or, possibly, about what has already happened to him. I know some reading this have already faced seeing their officer being significantly injured because of the world we live in and are facing the living nightmare of picking up the pieces afterward.

The storm is relentless right now, and it can be absolutely terrifying. Fear can do a number on your state of mind, which is why I think Satan pushes so hard to cause chaos and confusion. After all, faith and fear have a difficult time coexisting. That isn't to say I have not tried making them live together. There have been times where I say I have full faith that God has a plan, but also bite my nails as I wait for His plan to come to fruition. I confidently move in the direction God is pulling me, but also stop to have a panic attack every five minutes because I fear I'm not up to the task.

Faith and fear push and pull each other out of the way to take control of your attention. Fear tells you to stop moving because it's too scary, while faith convinces you to trudge forward, no matter what threats surround you, because you feel God telling you to do so.

A great example of this is the story in the gospel of Matthew that talks about Christ walking on water. Christ asked His disciples to take a boat and go ahead of Him to the other side of the water while he dispersed the crowd after the miracle of feeding the 5000. The scriptures say the boat was a considerable distance from shore[20] when Christ began walking on water toward them. They were afraid at first, but He then said, "Don't be afraid, it's me!" Peter asked, "If it's really you, ask me to come to you." Christ did. Peter then got off the boat and began walking on the water toward Jesus[21]. Peter was miraculously able to walk on the water, as promised.

However, when his attention shifted from Christ to the wind and the waves around him, he got scared. He thought of the potential danger of the storm, took his attention off Christ and His power, and in doing so, he began to sink. Like any of us can probably relate to, he panicked and cried out for help[22]. When Christ pulled him back up out of the water, I like to imagine His admonition is soft and said with a smile, as if to say, "Couldn't you see I was here the whole time?"

In the storm you currently face, there is plenty to be afraid of. There is the howling wind of insults toward police officers. There are the lightning strikes of riots. There are the thundering waves of hatred rolling forward unchecked by fact or truth, taking down anyone who dares question them as bigots or racists - even when the facts in question have nothing discernible to do with either of these things. There is the pelting rain of police officers being blamed for everything bad in society. It is a hell of a storm.

Through all of this, however, God reigns supreme. He always has and He always will. This can be hard to keep in mind, though.

---

[20] Matthew 14:24
[21] Matthew 14:28-29
[22] Matthew 14:30

With how loudly the anti-cop crowd cries out against your spouse and everything important to you, it can be easy for fear to push faith out of the way and make you a nervous wreck. With so much commotion, it can be hard not to fret about what you see around you. Chaos is an amazingly effective tool of the Devil because it threatens to edge out the peace God can give you. It causes confusion, pain, and anger, all of which can knock you off balance and make you fight to regain your grip on truth.

The fact is, however, that God knows all. He sees all. He is all-powerful. That knowledge isn't just something that can give you comfort. It is something you can truly draw power from when you take Him at His word and choose to live according to those promises. After all, think about everything God has done for you before. Think of the storms you've been led through prior to this: the storms in your marriage, in friendships, or in your own mind, each one teaching you and building you up with the strength you need for the next. Think of the promises God has made throughout the scriptures and to you personally, keeping in mind that He cannot lie to you. Think of others He has led through seemingly impossible circumstances and remember that He loves you just the same.

Just like Peter, you do not have control over the storm. You have no control over the actions of others. You cannot control whether people believe in the good of the majority police officers or not. You cannot change what the media reports. You have no control over what kind of people your husband interacts with while he is on shift. You cannot control the traffic, or the weather, or basically anything else in the world around you. If you have been a police wife for a while, you realize you scarcely even have the ability to plan if your officer will make it home for dinner or bedtime or not. There is an awful lot that's out of your control.

On the other hand, there are plenty of important things that are in your control. You have full control over what kind of person you are and how you respond to others. You get to control what kinds of behaviors, messages, and attitudes you spread out into the world. You get to control what kind of a relationship you have with God[23] with how often you pray and seek His guidance and how closely you follow it. You get to control what kind of wife you want to be to your officer. You get to choose how you spend your days - whether you idle away the time God has given you or use it to your full advantage.

Most importantly, you get to control where you focus your attention. If you feel afraid of the world, for your safety or for your officer's, you can choose to lift your eyes to Christ instead of wallowing in that fear. You can choose instead to focus your attention on God and His promises. You can lift yourself up through meditating on His word, reading stories of others who were delivered through their faithfulness, listening to uplifting music, or praying. Reject the temptation to sit and dwell on all the bad things that could happen to you and instead, focus on the faithfulness of God.

Far from denying your feelings, this is more about re-framing them. It is natural that negative things will get under your skin at times. God made us as we are, emotions and all. Even though it can hurt at times and you might wish you didn't feel that hurt,

---

[23] James 4:8

48

they are not an inherently negative thing. Feeling sad, hurt, angry, afraid, upset, jealous, or any combination of these drives you to seek comfort. Knowing that you are a child of God means that you know where you can turn to feel better. You can take comfort knowing He is always going to be there to provide the help and guidance you need, just as any loving Father would.

When you start to worry, try not to focus on the potential danger. This can be done by adjusting the way you pray. Praying to ask God not to let something happen is normal, but it can be helpful to change those prayers into asking for what you would like to happen. For example, when you ask that God will not let your husband be in danger this shift, the natural next step is to think about all the dangers you would specifically like God to keep him safe from. Instead, ask for God to bring your husband home safely, then picture what it will be like to hold him again. Express gratitude for the opportunity you have been given to love such a brave and selfless man. Pray that he will be able to depend on his training in tough situations and that he will have the discernment necessary to keep himself and those around him safe.

When you pray for these things, picture them having already come to pass. Believe that you have already received those things, and they will be yours[24]. Instead of wondering how and when God will make it happen, affirm that God will give you the wisdom and guidance you and your officer both need. Resist the urge to think about the worst outcomes, and instead, think about the goodness and sovereignty of God.

---

[24] Mark 11:24

Knowing that God is for you gives you the freedom to live without fear. It gives you the freedom to know that after you've done all you can do, God is able to make up the difference. You can take comfort in knowing that no matter what happens, God is there. No matter what persecution you face, no matter what danger you or your family may find yourselves in, no matter what tragedy may come your way, you can know for sure that your Father is watching over you. You can trust that He is making the way ahead of you, clearing out obstacles before you even know they exist.

You can be comforted in the knowledge that He is working absolutely everything you encounter for your ultimate good - even when those things make your heart feel like it's going to drop into your stomach. He can provide peace when He leads you through tough times, even if it's not right to take you out of those tough times right away. He will be there in your darkest moments, ready and willing to take you by the hand and lead you to your next step.

We do not have control over any of it happening. When you give into that lack of control and know you have a God who is in control, who loves you and your family, and knows more about what is going to happen than you do, you can relax a little. When you make the choice to trust His goodness and ultimate control, it allows you to ignore the storm raging around you knowing with all your heart that He will save you when you reach out your hand, every single time.

No matter what trouble you face, you can rest easy in the peace of the Lord. Even in the worst life can bring you, He is there.

His sovereign hand guides you and protects you until that day when you meet Him again and hear the phrase, "Well done, thou good and faithful servant."[25] Our present sufferings are nothing in comparison with the glory that awaits us[26]. I truly believe that, and earnestly look forward to that day.

Even though the opposition of the world is so loud, so persistent, and practically unavoidable right now, it amounts to nothing compared to the power of God. God is there for you, unrelentingly, in the brightest moments and in the darkest, forever working in your favor. With God by your side, you are stronger than the enemy could ever imagine.

---

[25] Matthew 25:23
[26] Romans 8:18

# PRAYER IDEAS

- Express gratitude for the promises that God gives you of safety and a plan for the future.
- Thank Him for His presence with you in this storm and always.
- Ask for help discerning what you can control and what you cannot.
- Ask to know what you need to do to take action on the things that are within your control.
- Ask to feel at peace about the things that are not in your control through the knowledge that He will take care of them.

# LOVE YOUR ENEMIES

*You have heard that it was said,*
*'Love your neighbor and hate your enemy.'*
*But I tell you, love your enemies*
*and pray for those who persecute you,*
*that you may be children of your Father in heaven.*
*Matthew 5:43-44*

Sometimes, loving your enemies sounds like a really bad joke. Even in the best of times, it can be a struggle. Right now, however, the enemies of law enforcement are more ferocious than ever.

Whether they are calling you a "bootlicker", harassing you, damaging your personal property, or flooding your inbox with nastygrams, those who hate the police are everywhere. We have to see our loved ones being dragged through the mud, accused of playing a part in some of the most atrocious of evils

Individuals are not the only guilty ones, either. There are whole corporations that stand with the worst kinds of criminals and against the police. Every time you turn on the television, you are inundated by another message about how bad the police are and how they need to be reformed. Sometimes this propaganda is disguised as a fight for justice, and sometimes it is promoted outrightly against law enforcement. Seriously, reach out an arm and you will certainly brush against someone willing to decry the police.

When all this is happening around you, the idea of loving your enemies can understandably make you feel a little prickly. It can be hard to even like others right now, let alone love them. After all, it's really easy to love the people who are nice to you. If someone brings you gifts all the time, tells you you look good today, and praises you all the time, it's pretty easy to have warm fuzzy feelings for them.

When people are rude to you, though, your natural inclination is understandably different. Annoyance, bitterness, and hatred come to mind a lot more easily than compassion and understanding when we are hurt. God, however, calls us to do what is right, not what is easy. He calls us to do the things that will change ourselves and the world. Loving your enemies, for better or worse, is one of those things.

That being said, it's still hard. How, exactly, are you supposed to love others when they can be so insufferable?

First, remember who you answer to. In the end, you have no responsibility to answer to your enemies. You don't really have to answer to your friends and family. Ultimately, you have to answer to God.

What God wants from you is to carry yourself with dignity and strength[27]. You have nothing to prove to anyone. You are under no responsibility to prove that law enforcement is 99.98% good or that riots are bad or that they have their facts all wrong or that they're interpreting statistics incorrectly or that their source is inaccurate or not credible. You only have to act in a way that proves that you are Christ's disciple. Your actions prove who you are, not what the other person deserves.

When you consistently treat others with love, regardless of what they do to you, you set yourself apart as a person with integrity. You prove to the world that, no matter what is done to you, you will side with God and do what He asks of you. That kind of courage is in short supply in this day and age, meaning it's even more impressive to find. Remember: no matter what someone has done to you to deserve something bad from you, people will remember what they do and what you do in their own right. Your politeness reflects on you, not them. Similarly, their vulgarity reflects on them, not you - no matter how personal it can feel.

Second of all, remember the power that comes from loving your enemies. People who say the most hurtful things are usually in a lot of pain themselves. People who truly feel happy and secure in their current situation usually do not have the drive to make others miserable. As they say, misery loves company. When people are overcome with rage and have no healthy outlet

---

[27] Proverbs 31:25

for it, they will happily latch on to whatever cause they can, even if it misdirects that anger and hurt.

Loving your enemies, then, is the only way we can effectively change the world. When people feel how much you love them, even when they choose to act in a way that would totally justify a smack to the face, their defenses are more readily broken down. When others come to know how much you care, they will care much more about what you know.

Christ knew that, too. He knew that love changes the world: not anger, not snarky comments on Facebook, not memes, not facts, not brute force. Only love. The truth is, there's plenty of hurt to go around right now. Everyone is hurting. There are many in the media who stand to gain from people feeling lost, hurt, and broken, so they put forth narratives that serve to stir up those feelings. Whether your enemies have a legitimate reason to feel rage or not, in your opinion, their pain is real. As you navigate the war on cops, strive to remember that and act in love.

Fighting for what is right, by itself, will not win hearts. Standing for truth is essential, but doing so with love is the difference that will make the world a better place. Being loving toward others is what will change minds, little by little. Also, you can take comfort knowing that even if nobody changes their mind, at least God knows you tried. God is able to see the things you do and why you do them. In the end, everything you do is between you and God. When you stand with Him in the ways that matter most, you can know you will come out ahead.

Now that we have covered the why, let's get to the how. It's one thing to understand why God wants you to love your enemies, but it's another thing entirely to act on that knowledge. A powerful way to do so is to pray for them.

Even though praying is simple, doing so for your enemies is not necessarily easy. When you feel hurt by someone, praying for them is hard to imagine. Not long ago, I had the opportunity to learn this very well for myself. I was feeling hurt by someone when I felt the Holy Ghost remind me of the command to pray for my enemies. It spoke deeply to my heart - but I was, to say the least, not happy about it.

I had no interest in praying for my enemies, but I knew what God was asking me to do. I felt like a petulant child who was told to pick up my toys and did so while grumbling the whole time. I prayed and said something like, "God, I know you want me to pray for them. I don't want to. If I have to, I want to pray for bad things to happen to them." I sat for a moment, because even though the words weren't pretty, they were exactly how I felt. As my heart began to soften, however, I was able to adjust my prayer. I instead prayed, "Please help me know how to pray for them."

It was in that moment where I was open to suggestions that the Holy Ghost spoke to me. I was reminded that the person I was struggling so hard to love is also a child of God. They are also trying to find their way in a wicked, fallen world. Maybe they are doing so less gracefully than I am, but I would be hard-pressed to argue I am doing much better. I struggle, too. If I pray for bad things to happen to those who hurt me, I would have to be okay with others doing the same when I hurt them[28]. I know why I do the things I do, but others don't. If I want my mistakes to be handled with grace, I can't demand harsh condemnation for others.

With all this in mind, I felt the Holy Ghost teach me how to pray instead. I felt inspired to say: "God, please help them to have the experiences they need to become who you want them to be. I feel they're not there yet, but I know you've helped *me* see the light, so I know you can help them, too."

This prayer has shifted my whole life. I realized I don't necessarily need to see justice in the form of the people who have hurt me being hurt back. It doesn't make either of us actually feel better, but what would make me feel better is for them not to do it again - for them to join the side of God and not spread the work of the Devil anymore. A win like that is a win for everyone. I still struggle to pray for my enemies, but having this insight and a prayer like this in my back pocket gives me a really useful tool, a go-to perspective to revert to when I'm feeling challenged by someone.

Something that can be even more of a challenge than praying for your enemies is forgiving them. The reason forgiveness can be so difficult is because it is often so misunderstood. It feels like we're letting other people off the hook for what they've done. It doesn't feel fair.

However, that's not true. When you forgive those who have

---

[28] Matthew 7:2

hurt you, it doesn't let them off the hook. Whatever consequence is supposed to come their way will come, whether you hold on to your anger or not. Instead, forgiveness lets you off the hook from replaying that hurt over and over again.

Forgiveness doesn't mean that you think what they did was okay - simply that you love yourself enough not to let it ruin the rest of your day, week, month, or life. And maybe, just maybe, that you have the compassion necessary to see that they, like you, are imperfect people, trying to navigate an imperfect world, making mistakes along the way - just like you.

When we feel hurt, it is natural that we want to see the other person hurt, too. I mean, you see that in kids - if one hits the other, it is pretty normal for them to hit back. It seems only just that the person who made us suffer should also be made to suffer. The thing is, in seeking that vengeance, you have to put a lot of energy into making sure it happens. You either have to plan something yourself, which takes energy. If you don't seek out revenge yourself, you might find yourself obsessed with checking every so often to see if something bad has happened to that person. Maybe instead of checking in, you just sit and rage for a while when you think about them, hoping they'll get their comeuppance.

All of these things take away not from the person who hurt you but from your life going forward. It perpetuates what they have inflicted on you, rather than letting the damage be done and focusing on healing.

Forgiveness takes strength, even though it can feel like weakness. It feels like you're allowing others to get away with what they've done - and how is that fair?  When we're hurt, our natural inclination is to hurt that person back - like an emotional fight-or-flight response.  Responding with love and forgiveness feels like weakness, like we are exposing ourselves at a time we would most like to protect ourselves.

One of the greatest powers you have in your control is that of forgiveness.  Of refusing to carry the hurtful behavior of others around, of allowing God to deal with it in His own way and His own time.  Forgiving others does not mean their behavior was any less reprehensible, only that you have the faith to allow God to deal with it as He will and heal you in the ways you need most.

Forgiveness allows God to work in your heart and theirs. Because you don't have to fix their mistakes - God can do that. God sees everything they do, just like He sees what you do - along with the motivation behind it.  You never know how much people are hurting when they make bad decisions, but you don't have to.  You just have to be willing to acccept that God knows what's fair and will act accordingly.

Remember, however, that forgiveness also does not necessarily mean reconciliation.  You are under no obligation to be best friends with someone who has hurt you.  Forgiveness is a separate issue from deciding whether they should remain in your life or not.  I personally have relationships that have ended, but I've still forgiven that person.  I choose not to carry my anger or frustration with me and also choose not to make them part of my life anymore.  It isn't about punishing them.  Instead, it's about having the boundaries that allow me to protect myself and my family from harm.

Being hurt by others is an unavoidable part of this life. Find the strength to pray for those who hurt you. Start small if you have to. As you work on it, your prayer muscles will expand and get stronger. You will get better and more effective at praying for your enemies, just like God has asked you to do. Doing so is not easy, but getting into the habit is completely worth it for the peace of mind it brings you.

Even though loving your enemies can be one of the hardest acts of faith you can encounter, it is also the thing that can best refine you and help you become more like Christ. The overwhelming presence of enemies right now is a difficult place to find yourself, but you can use this difficult time to teach you more than you could have ever learned otherwise.

# PRAYER IDEAS

- Express gratitude for the love God shows you - especially the love He has for you when you least deserve it.

- Express gratitude for everything you have personally been forgiven for.

- Ask God to forgive those who have hurt you, and ask for help in doing the same.

- Recognize that forgiveness is about the healing God has to offer you, not about letting others get away with things.

- Ask for help mending what has been broken by the actions of others.

- Pray about how to pray for your enemies and what they need most, understanding that they are likely doing the best they know how to do.

- Be frank with God about your struggles in this area - this is not an easy thing to do! Your effort to do so means as much to Him as your success.

- Commit to praying regularly for your enemies, even (especially) when you find it most difficult.

# GUARD YOUR HEART

*Above all else, guard your heart,*
*for everything you do flows from it.*
*Proverbs 4:23*

With all the negative things happening in the world, it comes as no surprise your heart is in serious turmoil. At turns, you might find it feels heavy. Maybe it feels bruised. Sometimes it feels like a vice is gripping it. Whether you find yourself reading about another police shooting, rioters burning down more cities, more anti-cop rhetoric spewed by a family member you previously believed to be on your side, or you find yourself weighed down under the cumulative impact of these kinds of things, you are going through a lot lately. As a result, now, more than ever, you have to be sure to guard your heart.

The top reason this is so important is that everything you do is impacted by the state of your heart. When anger and hatred are allowed to take root in your heart, everything you do comes from a place of hurt. Having patience for your family becomes more difficult. Choosing good things that nourish your soul and body is more of a struggle. Just managing your daily chores can become a slog when you are nurturing negativity in your heart.

The state of your heart affects how you look at things. When you consume media that tells you all about the wickedness of the world, you end up looking at the world through gloom-colored glasses. When you allow anger into your heart unchecked, that anger will flow out at others, even those who didn't play a part in making you angry in the first place.

On the other hand, when you find peace in your heart, you can react to others from that place of peace. While being hurt is sometimes unavoidable, tending carefully to your heart can help lessen how much the negativity of others impacts you. Doing so can not only help you thrive during trying times like these, but also allows you to be a light to the world. Nurturing your heart allows you to reserve the mental energy you need to take care of others.

Guarding your heart can be tough, however. We live in a day and age with unprecedented access to news from all over the world. You can learn about a breaking story pretty much the moment it happens and follow it as it unfolds; and from multiple perspectives, no less. The first and most important aspect of guarding your heart, then, is in learning how to protect it from superfluous negativity.

Having the ability to know about everything in the news at a moment's notice does not mean you are required to do so. After all, everything you read, listen to, witness, and take part in affects the state of your heart. When you overload yourself with all the bad news the world has to offer, your heart is naturally impacted and often negatively.

You have to decide for yourself where the line is between being properly informed and needlessly overwhelmed. You may consider deleting the news app from showing on your phone. You might block news sources from your Facebook feed - or take a break from social media altogether. You may ask your husband to give you the highlights of the news if he's more emotionally equipped to handle it. Maybe you can find a specific podcast host to follow daily to know what's happening without an endless deluge of negativity - bonus points if you find one with a good sense of humor to help you diffuse extra tension.

When considering where the line is between helpful and hurtful amounts of news, consider how it makes you feel. Is the news you are reading or listening to helping you feel empowered to make positive changes in your immediate environment, or is it making you feel helpless and hopeless?

Sometimes, what you read or watch in the news makes you depressed, but there is often nothing you can do about it. Those things, ultimately, are a waste of your mental energy. They take away from you, needlessly and negatively impacting how you do the things that really matter. If those things do not empower you to make a positive change, they represent a waste of mental energy. What good is it to know all the bad stuff in the world if you don't then have space in your heart to focus on your kids and your husband? On the wonderful things you have in your life that God has given you to enjoy?

It's not about living in a bubble. Blocking out every single bad thing in the world is not possible, nor even necessary. In fact, you need to know some of the wickedness so that you can both avoid those things and also make positive changes. Think of guarding your heart more like keeping it in a greenhouse: you block out what can kill the good seeds in your heart, and you let in what will help it grow.

Nourish your heart by listening to audiobooks or podcasts about people who inspire you to do better. Paint beautiful pictures. Listen to beautiful music that gives you goosebumps. Do nice things for other people. Do whatever things make your heart feel like it's going to burst at the seams. The more you build up your heart with the awesome things God has provided for you, the better it will be able to withstand the evil this world has to offer.

Another important aspect of guarding your heart is turning to God. Consistently turning to God helps you get the spiritual rest you need. When you live at a time where you can find more misery everywhere you turn, God can give you rest that goes far beyond the things of this world. God is the only one who knows exactly what you're going through. He sees you, even when you find yourself lost in the valley of the shadow of death. He knows the truth of all things, even when you face things that make it feel like the truth doesn't matter. No matter what potential destruction you envision for your future, He is the only one who knows whether it will come to pass or not. More than ever, you need to make sure God is a part of your life with a few key habits.

First of all, think about your prayer habits. As often as possible, speak to God like you would a friend. Tell Him all the things that are bothering you and why. Express gratitude for the amazing things He has already given you. Ask for help coming up with solutions to help you feel better. Request His guidance in finding friends who can help you. Even if you find yourself struggling to express yourself eloquently, He wants to hear from you. He is your Father, and as such, He is anxious to help you with whatever you need. This is especially true when you find yourself in such difficult times. The more you make prayer a part of your life, the better you will get at hearing His voice and seeing His hand in your life.

Next, work on getting into the habit of reading God's word every day. Whether you make a goal of reading one chapter or several pages per day, immersing yourself in the scriptures will help you know what to do each day to help yourself and your family through this difficult time. How you do it is a completely personal matter. I have trouble focusing on scriptures unless I read from a physical copy and take notes with a pen and paper as I go, but you might find it more suitable to you to listen to an audio edition of the Bible while you walk your dog in the morning, or use a Bible app to read and notate on your phone while you nurse your baby - which is something I have had to do before to actually make time for it! However you do it, when you make it a habit and open your heart up to God's influence on a regular schedule, you have a much greater ability to know what He needs you to do.

With all the stress you face, it's also important to make sure you are managing your emotions in healthy ways. This is especially true when it comes to anger. One scripture that resonates with me is Ephesians 2:26-27, which says: "In your anger do not sin: Do not let the sun go down while you are still angry, and do not give the devil a foothold." I personally struggle hard with anger. I frequently find myself saying things when I am angry that I have to apologize for later. I have definitely improved as I have gotten older, but anger is one of the most challenging emotions for me to manage. I think this is true for most people, actually, because anger is not something we talk about openly. It has so many loaded connotations that make it difficult to discuss.

The reason anger is so important to talk about is that it is powerful. Satan does not poke us, prod us, and stir us up to anger by mistake. He loves when we are destabilized by anger. Satan has nothing to do but work to bring you down, and he is extremely skillful at it. He knows that when our hearts are racing, our pulse is throbbing, when we have left our executive thoughts behind and descended into lizard brain where we can hardly see straight for anger, we are more easily persuaded to do things we would never do otherwise. Satan can very easily use that anger against you. This is precisely why he works so hard to poke at the very things that enrage us the most.

When spread unchecked, anger is at the root of the worst things in this world. Anger is what causes things like war and genocide. It lies at the heart of violent riots and the executions of police officers. Anger is the powerful force that can cause all kinds of widespread pain and destruction. Satan is well aware of that. He knows that anger is one of the fastest ways to push us down the path to sin and away from God. At a precarious time like this where the battle between good and evil is more evident than ever, you cannot afford to give into that anger. That's why one of the most powerful decisions you can make right now is to conquer your anger in healthy ways.

Remember that you can talk to God about everything you feel, even anger. You can tell Him just how angry you are about the protests, about the lies of the media, about attacks against police, and everything else that's getting you down. Tell Him how much it hurts to hear constant cries of imagined injustices. Cry it out, telling Him honestly how you feel, even if it just means you sit in His presence and cry. He will still be there, holding you, ready to pick you up, dust you off, and help you feel better.

I will admit, I used to feel uncomfortable about this. It felt wrong to go to God when I was mad because I was worried He would be offended. Trust me, though, that is not the case. God knows and sees everything. Your feelings of anger are nothing new to Him. He can take even your most unpleasant feelings and help you manage them in the best possible way.

That being said, you may not find yourself totally at peace after praying. There are other things you can do to dissipate your anger, also. You may find going for a run or getting some other kind of good exercise helps get you into a more relaxed state. Writing in a journal can be helpful - I know it helps me get to the root of the emotions I am feeling, which helps me process them better and make a plan to feel better. Sometimes, you might just need a good scream. If you live where nobody will hear you, go for it. If you are worried you will be called in for a welfare check, scream into a pillow or drive out somewhere in the wilderness and scream in your car.

Whatever you need to do to heal and guard your heart, be sure to make it a priority. Protect your heart from the things that make you feel helpless. Strengthen your heart against future trouble by reading God's word and praying to Him consistently. When you find yourself hurting the most, do what you can to lovingly nurse your heart back to health and allow God to help you do so. During the war on cops, more than ever, it is up to you to ensure your heart is being taken care of in the best possible ways to make sure the impact you personally have on the world is the best it can possibly be.

# PRAYER IDEAS

- Tell God how grateful you are for the way He made you - emotions and all.
- Thank God for the heart He gave you and the love you have to offer the world.
- Acknowledge that your heart is the start of everything you do.
- Thank Him for helping you learn to express those feelings in a more healthy way.
- Pray to better understand how your heart needs to be protected - what you need to do to nourish it and what you need to guard it from.
- Ask for help guarding it against evil
- Ask for help managing your anger in better ways - ways that uplift you and others.
- Pray for help not being overwhelmed by those emotions and to be a better manager of them.
- When you're in the midst of feeling angry, pray for peace.

# STRENGTHEN YOUR MARRIAGE

*But Ruth replied,*
*"Don't urge me to leave you or to turn back from you.*
*Where you go I will go, and where you stay I will stay.*
*Your people will be my people and your God my God."*
*Ruth 1:16*

There is no doubt that the war on cops impacts your family life. When you and your husband are both under so much extra stress, you might find yourselves inclined to take it out on one another. You might have questions and disagreements about where to go from here, like whether he should continue in law enforcement or if maybe it is time to walk away.

That stress trickles down to your children, who you may find are acting out more than ever because they can sense your stress and have even less power over it than you do. When they are old enough to have some understanding of what is going on in the world, they can get scared. You might get scared about the things they are learning. It's scary to think about all the things they're exposed to. I heard a group of kids playing cops and robbers and was so triggered when I heard talk of, "Shoot the cop!" and I suggested we play something else - it hit just a little too close to home for my comfort, even though it was a completely innocent thing.

This is why I think the best advice anyone has given me has been from my mom. I called her one day when I felt particularly sad and stressed out, and she suggested that when the world feels crazy, you can take your power back by shrinking your world to those around you - by focusing on those that matter most. She encouraged me to resist the urge to look at all the scary things around me and, instead, take the best care of my family I can. After all, I can't control the world. Those around me will do what they are going to do. In the meantime, I can make the impact I need to where it matters.

God can take care of you in incredible ways, which has been covered in the past few chapters. In return, you can take care of your family. You might not be able to take care of all the people who are hurting right now. You might not be able to change the opinions or stop the actions of everyone who hurts others. You can, however, love your officer and your kids with everything you have. You can strengthen them for what they will face. You can help teach them the things they need to know to turn to God and be who they need to be for the rest of the world. By shrinking your world down, you take back the power you have and let go of the rest.

Best of all, when you focus your attention on your family, you can help make the most of these trials. By loving your family and helping each other get through the storm, you can become stronger individually and as a family. When you use this time to take stock of what works for you and what doesn't, you have the opportunity to use it for your good. You have the opportunity to cut the things out of your life that weaken your family, and increase the things that give you strength. By taking control of what matters most, you can use the war on cops and everything else going on in the world for the benefit of you and your family, rather that to your detriment.

The best place to start is in your marriage. Even in the best of times, your law enforcement marriage is stressful. Marriage in general is a refining experience, but when you add law enforcement into the mix, especially now, there is a lot of extra pressure. There is not only the unpredictable schedule and stress of the job but also the concern about ending up on YouTube or in jail for doing what he was trained to do. In addition, you still face the normal, everyday stresses of marriage. You probably still find yourselves annoyed by one another. You might both be a little more testy than usual. You might be more likely to snap at one another or assume the worst about one another.

Everything you face undoubtedly takes a toll on your marriage. Being intentional about your marriage, then, is even more important. If you want to make it through this storm with a good relationship with your husband, you must make that relationship a priority. Doing so ensures you keep the small negative things in check before they grow into big, hard-to-manage things. It means you can nurture the things that make you and your husband happiest. Most of all, it means you will have a happier, more resilient relationship with your husband, which will benefit you both no matter where this all takes you.

Because you are the one reading this devotional, this section will speak to your habits. Your husband has responsibilities, too, of course - but an improvement in your marriage has to start somewhere, so why not with you?

I know that loving your officer can be hard at times. He is not perfect, and when his stress increases, his behavior can make him harder to love. He might have habits that annoy you, be more likely to take things you say the wrong way, or just be less open to you and appreciative of the things you do. This is especially true when most police officers tend to close off about what's bugging them, meaning their lousy emotions come out in less than flattering ways. In those times, being lovey-dovey to your husband isn't the first thing that comes to mind. However, think about the verse in 1 John 4:19: "We love because He first loved us." God loves us perfectly, in spite of our many imperfections, which makes it easy to love Him. You can start the same pattern in your marriage.

At a time like this, being loving toward your husband is even more powerful. When you remind your husband you are on his side, no matter what, it can help strengthen him against the intense voices that speak out against him. It can help break down his defenses so he is more willing to open up to you, because he knows you are a safe place to land. That is a powerful thing.

This is not about being self-sacrificial. Loving your husband when he is difficult to love does not mean you have to lay down and accept bad behavior, but it can help you reframe it. Rather than taking his annoying behavior to heart, you can remember that he is having a hard time, too. Remember: people who hurt,

hurt others. Just as you might be inclined to take your frustration out on your husband, he probably has the same inclination. Someone has to start that change. Rather than hoping your husband does so, you can prompt the change first. You can take control of your attitudes and behaviors, and by so doing, influence his for the better.

Start by lifting up your husband in prayer. Thank God for the wonderful husband He gave you: for how brave he is, how selfless he is, what a good sense of humor he has, what a good father he is, anything and everything you love about him. Ask God to help him have victory over the areas where he is struggling. Ask to see your officer's heart and understand the pain behind any annoying or hurtful behaviors. When you find yourself really struggling with him, rather than complaining to a girlfriend about his shortcomings, rant and rave to God. You will likely walk away feeling better and with ideas of how to make things better. You can also pray for your husband to be able to see your heart. You can ask for help opening his eyes to how much you care and how hard you try to make things work for your family.

By immersing yourself in prayer, you will undoubtedly make your marriage stronger. When you address issues in your marriage prayerfully rather than operating off your gut instinct, you are better able to address the root issues in your marriage instead of squabbling about surface issues. You can communicate more effectively when God is in the mix because He sees both you as you truly are. He can bridge any gaps in understanding that exist between you and facilitate understanding. While it can be tough to face issues in your marriage, especially when facing the hatred of the world, fixing these things can only make your marriage stronger.

In your day to day life, do what you can to connect with your husband. Tell him how proud you are of him. Remind him how valued he is to you and your kids. Leave him cheesy love notes. Snuggle and watch ridiculous shows with him. Be intentional about feeding his heart and soul and reminding him how loved and appreciated he is at home. Plan dates with him (even if you need to also plan a backup date if it has to be canceled). Gross out your kids when he gets home. Take action with the time and energy you have to remind your husband that he is important to you. Remind him that you will stand with him after each and every hard day he has.

You may never have the perfect marriage. After all, you are both imperfect people - so trying to mesh those imperfections is not always pretty. However, when you do your best to come together in all circumstances, you can nourish your marriage. Even if you never achieve perfection, you can still grow it to be better and stronger. Make today count by loving your officer with all your heart, and you can face tomorrow knowing you have done the best you can in the time you had.

# PRAYER IDEAS

- Thank God for the marriage you have.
- Express gratitude for all the positive qualities you can think of about your husband.
- Thank God for the children He has given you and the opportunity you have to raise them.
- Ask for help knowing what they most need from you right now, and the time and energy to meet those needs
- Ask for help when talking about tricky subjects - finding the right opportunity to do so and having the right words when you need them.
- Pray for a deeper understanding of the things your husband does that are currently bugging you.
- Ask for God to help both of you overcome your bad habits and come closer as a couple.
- Ask that the trials you face together bring you closer together, not tear you apart, and ask for the knowledge of what you need to do to ensure that.

# RAISE UP YOUR KIDS

*Start children off on the way they should go,*
*and even when they are old they will not turn from it.*
*Proverbs 22:6*

Just as it is important to focus on strengthening your marriage during this hard time, it is equally important to make sure you are intentional about making time for your kids. After all, their mother and father are the most important teachers your kids can have. Even if you have kids who seem not to care what you think, whether it's because they are teenagers or toddlers (or, you know, children in general), they do.

What you teach them, both through your words and your actions, will impact them forever. At such a pivotal moment in society, your influence is now more important than ever. Again, even though this is the responsibility of both you and your husband, as you are the one reading this devotional, this section will primarily focus on your role as a mother.

Start simply by making sure you love on your kids every day. Set aside time to play with them, read with them, and connect with them. Go out and explore new places with them, whether the weather outside is sunny or stormy. Listen to them tell you stories about their day, even if you are bored to tears listening to Minecraft sagas.

Pray with gratitude for their strengths, especially when they can hear you doing so. Pray for the wisdom to help them understand and overcome their weaknesses. Open your heart to them and ask for the help you need to be the mother they need you to be. This can be tough to make time for, especially when you are feeling so stressed out, but it is a good thing to prioritize. It will help reduce stress in both of you. It will also help build the connection between you and your kids.

This connection helps you tackle the most difficult task you face right now, which is answering your kids' questions. They often hear way more about the turmoil in the world than you might like. It is sad to see the world your kids are growing up in and probably makes you wish they could stay little forever. As much as I wish it were, that's not an option.

Your kids cannot be confined to a protective bubble, away from all the bad things in the world. They are absolutely going to face adversity in life, both because of having a parent in law enforcement and because life, by itself, is just hard. Unfortunately, as a police wife, you know all too well how evil the world can be. You know the heartbreaking tragedies that happen to children. You have always been in a position of knowing too much and having to teach that information to your kids without scaring them.

As hard as it is to feel powerless over the state of the world, remember that you do have the power to prepare your kids. You can inform them - gently and age-appropriately - what they'll be facing when they go out into the world. You can help equip them with mental tools to not take it to heart. You can let them know what dangers are there and how to side-step them. You can explain to them how it hurts you, too, and give them tips on how you cope with it.

When the world looks bleak, you can hold them and let them cry it out until they're ready to face the world. While it's unfortunate that they will have to face hard times, it's also a blessing that they have you to endure it with them and help guide them through it.

Having a parent to guide you through hard times and explain to you what evil looks like is a huge benefit. Your children are blessed with a parent who is aware of the dangers of the world. When you distill that information into smaller, easier-to-handle tidbits of information, your kids will be better able to tackle the world ahead of them. The child who knows what evil they will have to face will not be caught off guard when it presents itself.

On the other hand, a child who is caught off guard by evil will not have the tools to know how to respond. When faced with something new and scary, they will be more likely to make a mistake. They will be more likely to be taken in by false ideas. If you haven't taken the time to be honest with your kids about even the hardest things they will have to face, they might not know if they can come to you about them. They might wonder if you know about those things or not. They might find themselves worried about scaring or disappointing you because they know about them.

If your kids have questions you find yourself unsure how to answer, pray about it. God can give you the words to say to help your kids learn what they need to know. After all, God knows not only their hearts, but also the things they will face down the road. He loves your kids even more than you do, which means you can trust Him implicitly with this. He can help you know what they are struggling with, how to calm their fears, and what tools you need to provide them with.

The most important thing you can teach your kids in this situation is the comfort that comes from God. You can teach them the power of prayer, whether it is to comfort them in the face of fears of fictitious monsters under their bed or actual monsters in the world. You can teach them stories of Bible heroes who overcame trials, too. You can show them what a good relationship with God looks like by strengthening your own relationship. You can show them how to love others courageously, even when they are unloveable. You can show them what being a disciple of Christ really means to you and inspire them to live in a similar way.

If you navigate this situation right, you will end up raising adults who are even better because of their hardships. The adversity your kids are facing right now can strengthen them for what they face in the future - because they will face adversity in the future, and when they are older, the stakes will be higher. Help prepare them now by leading them through this storm prayerfully. You can prepare them to be the change the world needs. You can strengthen them to always fight for what's right, no matter what opposition they face.

You can't make your kids' decisions for them, but you can put the scaffolding in place such that, when they have to make their own decisions, they will have lots of wisdom to draw on. When you do this, it becomes a part of them - and that is something they will absolutely never depart from.

In the end, God does not expect you to change the whole world, but to work within the environment He has placed you. With that in mind, make sure that in a world full of uncertainty, you do the best you can to take care of the family He has given you.

# PRAYER IDEAS

- Thank God for the children He has given you.
- Express gratitude for how your kids help you grow in faith, patience, humility, and anything else that comes to mind.
- Ask God to help you understand what your children need from you and how you can better meet it.
- Ask for opportunities to connect with your children and enjoy them.
- Ask for protection over your children in both mind and body from the evils of this world.

# NAVIGATING BETRAYAL

*"My relatives have gone away;*
*my closest friends have forgotten me."*
*Job 19:14*

One of the most painful things about the war on cops is the feeling when those closest to you betray you. I tend to forget about this between "resurgences" of cop hate, but inevitably, every time this kind of thing comes up, I have a new opportunity to discover how anti-law enforcement many of my beloved friends and family are.

Post after post rolls through my newsfeed from people in my kids' playgroups and other people I previously felt safe around. News headlines abound with stories of police brutality without being fact-checked, and every single one feels like a dagger to the heart – more so when posted by your aunt or your best friend. Every single one feels like the posters have forgotten all about who we are, choosing to believe the media rather than remembering the example we've shown them.

Hearing hatred from strangers is bad enough. When that negativity comes from those you love, when you start being "blocked" and disowned by people you value, it feels like your heart is being torn apart. It feels like such a personal affront, especially when they turn around and on the other hand say, "We're praying for your officer!" It can make you feel sick when you know what the spread of that negative information/opinions can be.

It feels like those you love most have turned their backs on you, your officer, and your kids because you know where all that hatred leads. You see the attacks against police officers that come as a result of all the false rhetoric, which makes those ideas terrifying. Even hearing someone say "Not all cops are bad!" can make you feel annoyed, as it still tends to imply that most cops are bad, except "that one guy I know."

All of this can grow feelings of distrust in your heart. Your friends and family are the ones you should be able to rely on, no matter what. They are supposed to have your back. When you see them spreading misinformation that could (in your imagination or in reality) lead to your loved one's death, it hurts. How could they do this to you? Don't they know what they are doing?

When it feels like those you are supposed to be able to most rely on have turned on you, it can make you wonder where you can turn. In such a scary world, where are you supposed to go with your troubles, if not your beloved friends and family?

In this circumstance, you might find yourself identifying with the story of Job. Job was a wealthy, righteous man with lots of livestock and a big family. Satan suggested to God that the only reason Job was so righteous was because he had everything he could ever want - so why wouldn't he be righteous? God did not believe so, so He allowed Satan to test Job mercilessly with everything short of taking away his life, basically.[29]

Satan was, as he usually is, ruthless. He began by taking away all ten of Job's children and his livestock, all in one day. Ouch. Yet, even in the depths of despair, Job worshipped God. Satan was not finished, however. Job was then afflicted with severe skin sores. Still, he would not turn against God, even though his wife encouraged him to. He found himself wishing he had never been born, but still, he did not turn against God.[30]

After that, Job is visited by friends who suggest that his suffering must be as a result of some unknown sin and is thus probably a deserved punishment. They similarly say that his children probably brought their deaths upon themselves. When Job gets irritated with them and essentially says they are useless liars, they get offended. Even though the criticisms from Job's friends don't dissuade him from following God, they still irritate him. He knows he is innocent and that God knows it, too. He wants to confront God about the injustice of his situation but finds himself unsure how to do so, considering he can't physically find God.

---

[29] Job 6-10
[30] Job 13-22

Eventually, God intercedes in the conversation between Job and his friends. When He does, He encourages Job to be brave in the face of all his adversity. He reveals to Job all sorts of evidence of His power, especially details about the Creation. As you might expect, Job is overwhelmed by the experience. He responds by acknowledging that God has unlimited power and knowledge, and that he himself does not. When God expresses displeasure at the questionable advice of Job's friends, Job even asks God to forgive them. God repays Job's faithfulness by restoring his health, property, and children.

The story of Job has a lot of inspiring messages for facing adversity, including how he dealt with his friends. After all, his friends seem like huge jerks. I mean, they are talking to a friend of theirs who has lost everything and is in mourning, and they tell him he probably did something to deserve it. Even though Job does not cast them out of his house or anything, he becomes irritable, sarcastic and impatient with them. Understandably so: I have done the same. Navigating relationships with frustrating people is difficult, even when they are people you would generally do anything for.

One thing you have to remember is that your loved ones are human. They make mistakes. They are unlikely doing things just to hurt you. Dealing with other's imperfections is tough, but if you can remember they are imperfectly doing the best they can, it can help. After all, the negative information against police pervades the news media. While there are some people who are just evil and want to do bad things, I think most of the anti-cop crowd genuinely have good intentions but don't know better. You could call it naive to think that way, and I get it.

On the other hand, maybe that's healthier – or at least less stressful – than believing everyone is out to get you. I think most people have the desire to make the world a better place, not burn it to the ground - even if those who burn it to the ground get more attention from the media.

You also have to remember that Satan is really good at deceiving people. He is the father of all lies[31] and has been from the very beginning when he convinced Eve to eat the fruit in the Garden of Eden. He is the one who drove Cain to kill Abel, who convinced the builders of the tower of Babel it was a good idea, and compelled those who nailed Jesus to the cross to do so. Remember that.

Satan is really good at laying difficult-to-discern traps. Those who become entangled in his traps are not inherently bad people. Sometimes those traps are more about fear of retribution than wholehearted belief, too: It's a scary world out there for anyone affiliated with law enforcement, and at times, I can't blame my loved ones for distancing themselves from it as far as they can get. When you find compassion for those who have been misled, you can have a bigger impact on them. I know that is a lot easier said than done, but remember: judgment and condemnation causes more hurt, which means they are less likely to change their minds.

In these circumstances, do your best to temper your emotions and give your loved ones the benefit of the doubt. All of us are imperfect and emotion-driven. Do your best to be the bigger

---

[31] John 8:44

person. Refuse to let anger dictate how you interact with those you love most in the interest of not alienating them. When you have conversations about this sensitive topic, remember to be polite. Be respectful. Most importantly, whenever possible, have conversations in person, not on Facebook or via text message. In person, you get the benefit of tone of voice and body language, where you don't get those things in written language. That barrier can cause a bigger rift than necessary. If you want to retain the relationship, it's best to talk about sensitive things in person.

That being said, setting boundaries with friends and family is okay - and necessary. You can refuse to discuss these things with them if you feel it will devolve into petty arguments. You can unfollow or mute them on social media without unfriending them, and they don't even receive a notification about it - hooray! You can do what you have to do to protect the peace in your heart and the peace of your family.

You can shut down anti-cop sentiments when they start, telling them you won't entertain those ideas - politely, of course. Enduring this situation with grace does not mean you are obligated to endure abuse. When it becomes necessary, you are welcome to walk away from discussions without trying to get the last word or change minds.

As with all things, however, be sure to do all the boundary-setting prayerfully. God knows well who needs to be in your life and, conversely, whose life you need to play a role in. If someone hurts you, don't immediately remove them from your life without really considering it. In most cases, a cooling off period from that person can do wonders after things get overly heated. After all, disagreeing with others is okay. Feeling upset and angry with others, even those you love, is also okay. Take things day by day, and make big decisions about relationships by the Spirit.

Of course, no amount of boundary setting in the world will prevent the cold, hard fact that during the war on cops, you will probably lose friends. You may also become more distant from family members. I understand these things very well, as we have personally experienced both. It hurts. It's hard when people show themselves to be different than you thought they were. It's painful when they trust the lies and deceit of the media over their personal knowledge of your character.

When that happens, take the time you need to grieve. This is a loss just like any other, and it is okay to feel sad. It's okay to feel right about removing toxic influences from your life but also feel sad about it.

Regardless of what boundaries you end up setting, regardless of whether they're mild fences or hard-and-fast letting people go from your life, remember to pray for those you disagree with, just as you would your outright enemies. Pray for both of your hearts to heal and to make the right choices for the long run rather than letting emotions rule over what matters most. Assume the best, do what you feel God leading you to do, and let Him take care of the rest.

You may also find that the war on cops makes it more difficult for you to make and keep friends. When the time comes where it feels like everyone you know and love is against you and those you love most, it can put you in a more self-protective state. You may find yourself being more judgmental toward others in order to keep them at a safe distance where they can't hurt you.

Satan loves this. He loves when your fear of being hurt keeps you away from others who you could make a difference with. That is not to make you feel guilty or ashamed, but to be aware of one of the many traps he can ensnare you in. By being aware of this pitfall, you can make courageous choices. Sometimes just having the courage to let yourself be vulnerable enough to make a friend can be a really hard thing, but God can and will guide you in this. You just have to be willing to let Him.

In a time like this, you definitely need friends. When you feel like you are losing friends and family left and right, it can be hard to think about that. I know there is a lot of hurt going around. It's hard to put yourself in a position to feel more hurt from people by being vulnerable. Do what you can to facilitate friendships with others.

If you find yourself having a hard time figuring out who you can count on and who you need to let go from your life, pray about it. Ask who needs to remain in your life. Ask who needs to be let go. Ask to be led to new friends who can uplift and encourage you. Listen to what God tells you. I know that that can be hard, especially when God asks you to maintain a relationship you are feeling hurt in. Trust Him. Talk to Him. Come to Him. He will let you know what you are supposed to do and can soften your heart and heal it as necessary.

Take comfort in knowing that Christ experienced betrayal, too. He knows all too well how you feel, and then some. When you feel the most isolated, remember that you are absolutely not by yourself in this. He has been there, done that, and he has the scars to prove it. No matter what happens to the relationships between you and your loved ones at this time, take heart knowing that you have a perfect, loving God on your side who knows your heart and will never, ever leave or forsake you.

# PRAYER IDEAS

- Express gratitude for the good friends and family members He has given you.

- Thank Him for the opportunities hurtful friends give you to grow and learn what not to do in a friendship.

- Ask for help finding friends who will uplift you, strengthen you, and make you an all-around better person - and who you can help do the same.

- Request help in nurturing the good friendships you have.

- Pray for discernment about which friends should be eradicated from your life and how to do so gracefully.

# PUT ON THE KEVLAR OF GOD

*Finally, be strong in the Lord and in His mighty power.*
*Put on the full armor of God, so that you can take your stand*
*against the devil's schemes.*
*Ephesians 6:10-11*

I don't use the term "war on cops" facetiously or to be dramatic. I use it for good reason: you stand in the middle of a massive fight against good and evil. There are everyday battles you are required to fight in all kinds of battlefields.

You have to fight to keep your faith. You have to fight for good over evil, truth over lies. You have to fight to make sure your family is well taken care of and that you stay safe. As the wife of a law enforcement officer, you stand firmly in one camp - the side for law enforcement. When people learn who you are and what you stand for, at least on the surface, they may decide they hate you. They may find ways to attack your character, your beliefs, your husband, and basically everything you hold dear.

In this circumstance, the scriptural idea of the armor of God is incredibly powerful. Just like your husband gears up with Kevlar, guns, proper training, and a whole lot of intestinal fortitude, you need to gear up, too. You may not need to gear up with literal Kevlar and a gun, but with spiritual protection, as is spoken of in Ephesians 6:10-17:

> Finally, be strong in the Lord and in his mighty power.
>
> Put on the full armor of God, so that you can take your stand against the devil's schemes.
>
> For our struggle is not against flesh and blood, but against the rulers, against the authorities, against the powers of this dark world and against the spiritual forces of evil in the heavenly realms.
>
> Therefore put on the full armor of God, so that when the day of evil comes, you may be able to stand your ground, and after you have done everything, to stand.
>
> Stand firm then, with the belt of truth buckled around your waist, with the breastplate of righteousness in place,
>
> and with your feet fitted with the readiness that comes from the gospel of peace.
>
> In addition to all this, take up the shield of faith, with which you can extinguish all the flaming arrows of the evil one.
>
> Take the helmet of salvation and the sword of the Spirit, which is the word of God.

And pray in the Spirit on all occasions with all kinds of prayers and requests.

With this in mind, be alert and always keep on praying for all the Lord's people.

Even though Satan and all the lies that abound about law enforcement can feel unflinchingly powerful right now, God is and will always be more powerful. This metaphor of the armor of God is a great way to visualize how to equip yourself with all the power that God has to offer.

This passage begins by outlining what the armor of God can do for you. By putting on the armor of God, you can stand strong against whatever danger may come your way. No matter what plots Satan can come up with, God can protect you. Whether they are general attacks on righteousness or attacks on your family because of your affiliation with law enforcement, doing so protects what is most important to you. When we know Satan is really good at coming up with ways to undermine your faith, it is especially important to do what you can to protect yourself from any and all attacks.

Note that this passage also highlights the fact that we are not battling one another, even though it can feel that way at times. Satan is the one stirring up contentions that drive people to do evil things. We fight against the powers of the spiritual forces of evil, first and foremost. This was discussed in the section on loving your enemies, but it's worth reiterating: Satan is really good at what he does, including taking down people who would otherwise be good.

The description of the armor of God itself begins with the belt of truth and the breastplate of righteousness. Always speak, do, and promote truth. Be an example of righteousness, so that no matter what anyone says about you or your family, you can stand strong and know that you are choosing to do the things God has asked of you. Choose to be Christlike in your dealings with others, to be honest and truthful, and to choose to do the right thing, no matter what anyone else chooses.

No matter what anyone else does to you, it is your decisions that show the strength of your character. It's in how we respond, not what happens to us, that matters to God. The breastplate of righteousness is also guarding your heart - after all, a breastplate protects exactly that. Choosing righteousness is part of guarding your heart, because it is preventing you from engaging in evil schemes yourself.

What comes to mind when discussing truth and righteousness is how confusing this time can be. We are inundated with more information than our minds can possibly process. There are facts and statistics and scientific experiments that seem to support whatever opinion people choose to have. There are statistics used both to prove police officers are good and that they're evil, depending on the context they're used in. There are even Christians who decry police officers as evil. There are generally evil people who support police officers, for reasons that may be for genuinely good or evil purposes. There are so many conflicting things out there it's not surprising if you find your head spinning.

All this chaos and confusion is like soul food to the devil. The enemy loves to make you doubt yourself, especially when you do everything you can to follow Christ. He loves to obfuscate the truth and make evil seem better than the good actually is[32]. After all, if he can lead people away even a little bit, he can continue to build on that doubt and lead them to bad places they never would have previously found themselves in. He loves to undermine the truths that can lead you to be a light for the world.

However, everything Satan means for evil, God can use for good. When you have questions and doubts and bring them to the Lord in prayer, you can become stronger than you would be otherwise. Receiving answers to these difficult questions can actually strengthen your faith and your resolve rather than destroy it. Just like building muscle, the challenge to your faith can help it become stronger than it ever could have become otherwise. When you come to God with your questions, you can take comfort knowing He will answer you truthfully[33]. Asking hard questions is not inherently an act of doubt. When you ask in faith, knowing that He will answer you, you are expressing your faith in His power to answer even the most difficult questions.

The description of the armor of God continues with an image of feet fitted with the readiness of the gospel of peace. You need to be mentally prepared for what you will face as a Christian police wife. You need to mentally be ready for battle; spiritually, emotionally, and physically, if necessary. Know what danger you might face and be prepared to react appropriately. If you know in advance how you will react to something, it will give you that much more of an advantage. After all, this is kind of like the

---

[32] Isaiah 5:20
[33] Matthew 7:7

training your husband goes through, isn't it? Fortunately for you, you do not have to be prepared with ten-codes and what to do if someone ambushes you during a traffic stop. You are more likely preparing for spiritual adversity - which I would personally take any day, I suppose.

Next, this passage instructs you to take up the shield of faith to extinguish the flaming arrows of the evil one. You can't prevent Satan from riling people up and shooting insults and challenges at you. He will do what he wants to do, and people will choose good or evil according to their will. That doesn't mean you are powerless to protect yourself, though. I love the visual in this passage of the shield extinguishing the arrows, preventing them from actually harming you. A shield is something you have to always carry, be aware of, and have at the ready. It is not a form of passive protection, something you just put on like a breastplate, but something you have to hold and use as active protection. You have to decide how much Satan's arrows will be able to hurt you.

You may not be able to choose if the arrows fly at you, but you get to decide if you take offense to them. You can decide whether to hold a grudge against those on the other side who attack you with those arrows, or whether you will forgive them and let that pain be put in God's hands. Even if the arrow hits you, you do not have to let the flames spread. If Christ is the living water[34], He is undoubtedly the best source of energy to extinguish the flaming arrows of the adversary.

---

[34] John 7:37

Next, the passage says to put on the helmet of salvation and take up the sword of the Spirit, or the word of God. These both sound like mental elements. After all, a helmet protects your head. Think about the helmet of salvation keeping your head pointed in the right direction as the world around you spins out of control, helping you to discern between what is truthful and what is not.

Sometimes making this determination can be difficult because Satan works really hard to mimic the things of God. For example, think about the Pharoah's sorcerers copying Moses and changing their rod to a snake, too.[35]. To a casual observer, the feats of power would have looked the same: up until the point where Moses's snake devoured theirs, anyway. You can hardly even blame those observers for being confused.

Satan loves when we're confused. He just loves to step in and offer us answers that lead us away from God. The only way to fight these attacks is to focus on the root of your salvation, to learn more about Christ and His ways and get to know His word intimately. Be knowledgeable about evil inasmuch is required to keep you safe from evil. Your intellect is an important thing. Having knowledge of both spiritual things and the things of this world, can help you make better decisions than you would otherwise.

Now, think about the comparison between the sword of the Spirit and the word of God. You might notice that, of all the equipment mentioned in the armor of God comparison, the

---

[35] Exodus 7:11

word of the Spirit is the only weapon mentioned. Everything else is armor.

This indicates that the word of God is your only true way to actively fight against Satan, while everything else is only defensive tactics. They are equally important, no doubt, but if you want to be an active participant in the fight for good, you can only do so through being intimately familiar with the word of God.

You can be better equipped with the word of God by making sure you get to know what He has to say. Get into a habit of reading the Bible, even a chapter a day. Get to know His word. Pray steadfastly to understand the things you struggle to understand. Get in the habit of reading it regularly, knowing what God truly stands for and what His Spirit feels like, and you will be better able to discern the good from the evil. Knowing God's word allows you to actively fight against attacks on it.

Lastly, this passage says to pray always and be alert. As a soldier on the battlefield would, look to your commander for orders. Ask God what to do, in every situation, then do what you are told to do. Pray for those around you and their health and well-being. Pray for your enemies, that they will come to know the truth.

Satan is relentless, which means you have to be just as relentless in your pursuit of righteousness. Be aware of the danger that could come your way. You don't have to be afraid of that, just be prepared to hold up your shield and stand your ground when necessary. It's kind of like how your husband never eats in a restaurant without facing the door: it's not that he is freaking out the entire meal, just that he wants to be alert and ready should any danger come his way.

In addition, pray for all who work for the cause of good, just like yourself, that you will be protected and guided the correct way. Satan is working just as hard against them as he is against you, so anyone who is working for good needs to be covered in prayer, too.

The danger around you during the war on cops can feel overwhelming, but by equipping yourself with the full armor of God, you can use the strongest tools He can give you to help keep yourself and those around you safe.

# PRAYER IDEAS

- Express gratitude for a scriptural guide to covering yourself in His protection.
- Acknowledge that He can protect you from all evil.
- Pray to know how to better protect yourself spiritually using the armor of God analogy.
- Pray specifically about the things that leap out at you while reading the description.
- Ask for help getting rid of unhealthy spiritual habits and replacing them with better, more protective ones.

# ALL THINGS FOR YOUR GOOD

*And we know that in all things God works for the good of those who love Him,*
*who have been called according to His purpose.*

*Romans 8:28*

This is not an easy time for law enforcement families. There is so much that does not make sense. There is so much pain. There is an incredible amount of unfairness. There are untold dangers we would never before have dreamed of.

I wish I could tell you without a doubt that things of the world will improve but frankly, I can't. I do not know that for a fact. I don't know what the rest of this time will look like, although the future predicted by Paul in Revelations looks pretty grim – at least until Jesus returns, anyway.

Still, nobody but God knows exactly how that will play out.

The same is true of your personal future. I do not know what you are being called to do. I have no idea what God needs from you and your family, only that He does have a plan for you. Of that, there is no doubt in my mind.

Maybe this is the end of the road for your family as far as law enforcement is concerned. If your officer feels it is time for him to walk away from law enforcement, maybe it is. Pray about it - and if it is, there is no shame in doing so. You have to do what's right for your family. You can take heart knowing you've done all you could, and now you get to move on and live a life that doesn't feel quite so dangerous. Enjoy it without feeling guilty - nobody blames you for doing so! If you are being called to move on, only God knows where you will go next – but I know it will be good.

Maybe you find yourself in the middle of things, feeling pulled between fighting to convince your officer to walk away or helping him to fight. Maybe you wish he would walk awa, but find it doesn't feel right. Maybe there's talk of your officer simply changing departments. I don't know. What I do know is that whatever uncertainty you find yourself facing, God will help you find your way. Keep trying to do what you feel is right, seek God, and rest in His promises, and you don't have to be afraid of the future.

Maybe you are at the very beginning of being a police wife and wondering what the heck you have gotten yourself into. Maybe you just started dating your officer. Maybe you've been married for a while, but your husband felt inspired to join and help make a difference. It is a heck of a time to join but more power to both of you. I know that with an undaunted focus on God, He will guide you in the issues that come with either of those circumstances.

Regardless of the particulars of where you find yourself, what I do know is this: You are where you are for a reason. Everything that has happened to you will be worked for your good - as will everything that may eventually happen to you. You will no doubt be changed by this storm, but I believe it will be for the better. You will become stronger. You will become smarter. You will learn more about the world, yourself, and your family than you ever could have learned otherwise.

By making sure to consistently pursue God, you can do your part to make sure that change will be for the better. Even if things don't seem like they are working out in your favor right now, trust that He can change that. When things are at their darkest, remember that He has told you He is the light of the world. Look to Him for the hope you need to live in this fallen world and return to Him, better than ever, having done everything He asked of you.

In the meantime, remember to take things one step at a time. I know how overwhelmed you feel, with all the extra anxiety and responsibilities on your plate. Don't think about tomorrow. Focus on today - right here, right now - and let the rest be in God's hands.

I know that can be easier said than done, but remember: worrying about tomorrow won't prevent anything bad from happening. It just means you have to suffer from that thing now and later if it does happen. No amount of anxiety has ever prevented horrific things from happening. Take the action you are able to take, then allow God to take the rest in His capable hands.

In this hard time, I would also like to encourage you to make sure you are taking care of yourself. If you find yourself deeply struggling, do not be ashamed to seek counseling, whether it's for yourself, for your marriage, or for your entire family. There is no shame in getting counseling! A qualified counselor will undoubtedly help you work through your personal struggles and give you more tools to get through this with your head above water. Just as God would suggest using a good doctor to mend you if you had a serious injury, He would encourage you to seek qualified mental health professionals to help you tackle the emotional wounds you face.

Through all of this, remember that you have a whole blue line family behind you. You are not in this alone, as much as the world might try to convince you of that. Again, even if this is the end of the road for your officer as far as law enforcement goes, you are both still appreciated for every sacrifice you've given - both by those on the blue line and God, who sees more clearly than anybody everything you have gone through. Your blue line brothers and sisters will still be here to support you, no matter what.

Seek out friends. Connect with others, as God has made us to be a social people. We need one another, especially when life gets its hardest. Get to know the wives in your department and learn from one another. Gain strength from one another. Get inspired by the stories each of you has lived. It can be hard to get out there, but make it a point to do so.

No matter where you go from here, continue to be undeterred in your pursuit of God. Cling tightly to Him and never let go, because you know that He will never tell you a lie or lead you astray. He loves you more than you can possibly imagine. Trust the promise that He does everything for your ultimate good — that even the worst, most heartbreaking things you find yourself facing right now will shape you into who He needs you to be. No matter what, God can help you find the good in the worst of situations.

You can and will make it through this storm. No matter how high the waves get, remember that the Savior is in your boat. Take heart, hold tight, and remember: this world will someday fade away. Someday, you will be back with Him. He will dry all your tears. If you have lived the way He asked of you, He will be able to tell you, "Well done, thou good and faithful servant.[36]"

On that day, I promise: this will all be 100% worth it. Continue toward God, pursue Him relentlessly, and do not ever give up. ♥

---

[36] Matthew 25:23

# ACKNOWLEDGEMENTS

I have so many people to thank for their help in getting this devotional written.

First and foremost, I am grateful that God led me here. I haven't always known why He has led me to where I am supposed to be, but I am grateful He trusted me enough with His message to try to write it out in this book. I'm grateful for every moment I've had with Him in prayer and through reading His word. I wouldn't be where I am today without His grace.

I'm also grateful to my husband for his support. Thank you for bringing me chocolate and a Coke when I'm having a rough day, without me even having to ask for it. Thank you for being there to encourage me when I'm feeling unsure of myself. Thank you for being an awesome father and letting me pursue my dreams, knowing our kids are in great hands. Oh, and thank you for making me turn off my electronics and watch dumb shows with you when I'm in a grumpy mood - I definitely need the reminder sometimes to let the other stuff go!

Thank you to my editor, Amanda, for being an amazing sounding board and making sure this book was the best version of itself before publication. I love being able to trust you with the words so near to my soul. I appreciate you so much, and your running commentary as you edited my words made me smile. Thank you for sharing your thoughts all around.

Thank you to our church family and everything you've done for our family in the past few years. You've watched our kids, you've brought us meals, you've listened to us cry, and you've given us encouragement when things seemed the most bleak. We can never repay you for what you've done, but hope someday we can sufficiently pay your service forward.

Thank you to my amazing launch team, including:

- Krystine Michaels
- Michelle Hill
- Autumn Slusser
- Tiffany Head
- Leslee Greene Parish
- Dee Torres
- Kim Crowley
- Julie Garcia-Williams
- Laci Lobbs
- Misty Hope
- Hayley Keller
- Alisha Cavin Sweyd
- Amanda Kelley
- Emily Evans
- Emma Johnson
- Amanda Yoder
- Hannah Lynn
- Lauren Hudson
- Shannon Williamson
- Nina Pyle
- Lori Rippole
- Kristina Russell
- Yolanda Coburn-Stinson
- Natalie Sarazin
- Suzanne Blackburn
- Kendra Pence
- Tiffany Lucille
- Kathy Spillers
- Sarah Nixon
- Kristin Cunningham
- Marcy Douglas
- Kimberly Gaouette
- Kara Fidd
- Amanda Kazzee
- Madison DiSanti
- Renee McMichael
- Katie Black
- Jenine Lewis
- Michelle Hill
- Jocelyn Small
- Heather Luke
- Jess Musacchio
- Ryan Bain

You all did so much to help me spread this message of hope and I am so grateful for you!

Thank you to all our local officers and the officers across America and the world for your service. Thank you to the families of officers who have fallen in the line of duty for your service and sacrifice. We see you, we love you, and we pray for you. To the families of all officers, I am so grateful for everything you do to support their pursuit of justice - especially in the face of such awful persecution. All of you are amazing, and I thank you for everything.

Finally, thank you, reader, for being the reason I do what I do. I hope I have been able to encourage you, no matter what you face. Thank you for your never-ending support!

# ABOUT THE AUTHOR

Leah Everly is the blogger behind Love and Blues Blog, where she helps police wives thrive in their difficult calling. When she's not busy writing, she can usually be found exploring outside with her kids or snuggled up with her nose in a book. She lives in Salt Lake City with her husband, a former police officer, and their children.

If you'd like to follow more of Leah's writings, visit loveandbluesblog.com. She is also on Facebook, Instagram, Pinterest, and Twitter under the handle @lovebluesblog.

# OTHER DEVOTIONALS
# BY LEAH EVERLY

**The Proverbs 31 Police Wife:** "She is clothed with strength and dignity, and laughs without fear of the future." Be honest: does that sound like you? If not, you aren't alone. Being married to a police officer is not easy, especially in today's world. Everything about your future can feel extremely uncertain, and not just when it comes to your officer's safety. Stress caused by facing unexpected day-to-day issues while tackling solo parenting, unpredictable shifts, and general loneliness tends to wear on you after a while.This makes emulating the traits of the Proverbs 31 wife even more important for police wives. Striving to be more like the woman described in these verses will help you increase your faith, find more peace, reduce overwhelm, and generally live a happier and more fulfilling life, no matter what troubles come your way. This devotional will help you develop those traits by teaching you how to team up with God in every aspect of your police wife life.

**Refuge: A Spiritual Guide To A More Peaceful Law Enforcement Home:** Being married to a police officer is hard. That might be especially true as a Christian. The idea of being in the world, but not of the world, seems particularly hard as your husband faces the worst of the world, then comes home and has to be the loving father and husband his family needs. Those struggles are what makes turning your home into a refuge that much more important - and that much more powerful. This devotional is all about finding ways to make your home a more peaceful, gospel-centered place for you, your officer, and your children to come home to. It could just make all the difference in the world.

Both devotionals are available on Amazon.

**Interested in learning about future devotionals?** Be sure to visit loveandbluesblog.com and sign up to Leah Everly's weekly newsletter to be the first to hear about upcoming projects!

# COULD YOU DO ME A QUICK FAVOR?

As a self-published author, reviews are the *most important* tool I have of making sure my books get into the right hands.

If you have been inspired and uplifted by this devotional and want to help other police wives find out about it, I would so appreciate if you would take your time and write about your experience in a starred review on Amazon or Goodreads (or both, if you feel so inclined.)

Of course, you can share it with your friends, too – both of these help spread this message of hope far and wide!

Regardless of which you choose, thank you for reading this devotional and taking the time to help spread the message.

Have an awesome day!

Love,
Leah

UNSHAKEABLE

Made in the USA
Monee, IL
14 May 2021